Life's Meandering Path

A Secular Approach to Gautama Buddha's Guide to Living

Karma Yeshe Rabgye

Foreword by Ted Meissner
Secular Buddhist Association

Copyright © Karma Yeshe Rabgye 2014
All rights reserved.
No part of this publication may be reproduced, stored in a retrieval system, or transmitted, in any form or by any means, electronic, mechanical, photocopying, recording, or otherwise, without the prior permission of the author.

Karma Yeshe Rabgye asserts the moral right to be identified as the author of this work.

ISBN: 1500618942
ISBN 13: 9781500618940

To my sisters, Denise and Lynne, for always being there for me.

You can read more from the author and follow him on Facebook and Twitter by going to www.buddhismguide.org.

Contents

Foreword		xv
Introduction		xix
1	Truth is Found in Stillness	1
2	It's All in the Tea Leaves	22
3	The Mangala Sutra	31
4	Foundation Principles	34
	1—Avoid people exerting a negative influence	34
	2—Associate with people exerting a positive influence	37
	3—Show respect to those who have earned it	40
	4—Live in a suitable location	42
	5—To have done good deeds in your past	43
	6—Be on a suitable path	47

5	Supporting Principles	52
	7—Have good learning skills	52
	8—Have good practical skills	54
	9—Follow a code of discipline	56
	10—Practice appropriate speech	68
	11—Support your parents or guardians	72
	12—Take care of your spouse and children	74
	13—Have an appropriate livelihood and balanced life-style	76
6	Social Principles	84
	14—Be charitable	84
	15—Practice virtuous actions	88
	16—Help your friends and relatives	91
	17—Be blameless in your conduct	94
	18—Refrain from harmful acts	96
	19—Great effort	103
	20—Refrain from intoxicants	111
	21—Be diligent in your practice	112
7	Individual Principles	117
	22—Venerate those worthy of it	117
	23—Be humble	120
	24—Be content	123
	25—Be grateful	126
	26—Receive teachings at a favourable time	128
	27—Have patience	133
	28—Giving and listening to advice	137
	29—Have a teacher	140
	30—Discuss the teachings	150

8	Refining Principles	154
	31—Practice self-restraint	155
	32—Understand the four truths	162
	33—Follow the eightfold path	186
	34—Work towards freedom from suffering	218
	35—Be unaffected by worldly conditions	225
	36—Understand impermanence and nonself	233
	37—Free yourself from defilements	247
	38—Achieve lasting peace and true happiness	255
9	The End of the Road	264

Life's Meandering Path

Om, may all become happy,
May all become free of illness,
May all see what is auspicious,
Let no one suffer!

Foreword

IN ITS 2,600-YEAR history, Buddhism has continually evolved to suit the environmental conditions in which it has found itself. Core principles of the Four Truths remain a constant, along with the underlying poisons of greed, hatred and delusion as foundational contributors to our dissatisfaction in daily life, as do their remedies so brilliantly articulated as the Eightfold Path. With each new culture it encounters, Buddhism finds resonance in our shared human experience of suffering and the possibility of its attenuation and eventual extinguishing. Far from being damaging or a watering down of Buddhism, this has allowed the tradition to grow, flourishing with new and distinct branches. Without that planting of Buddhist seeds in new and fertile soil, the world would have been deprived of the unique pragmatic quality of Zen, or the wondrous beauty and wisdom of Vajrayana, the third commonly recognized traditional school we see from our Tibetan brethren.

It is not surprising, then, that a secular approach is becoming recognized as a unique and distinct branch of Buddhism. Rather than having a critical dependency on the validity of the practice being based on a supernatural belief system, Secular Buddhism focuses on a naturalistic interpretation of the Dharma. Secular Buddhism opens the door for participation, setting aside ideological narratives about other worlds and lifetimes in favour of that which is shared by all humanity, our common experiences, trials and joys in daily life, as people rather than as Buddhists.

There is an understandable aversion by many to the term 'secular', which can often be interpreted as being in opposition to the sacred. As with many criticisms, such problems can be resolved by an open exploration of what is meant by 'secular'. Though it can and often is viewed as a rejection of sanctity, Secular Buddhism meets people where they are, honouring that as human beings we are all deeply moved, inspired and energized by that which we find to be meaningful. There are many kinds of Secular Buddhists, those who light incense, bow and find a spiritual value in the practice as it positively impacts them and those around them, all within this natural world.

Karma Yeshe Rabgye has written *Life's Meandering Path* to nurture what we do as people rather than what we must believe to be Buddhists. His selection of the Mangala Sutra is brilliant in that it relies on that very notion: that the teaching and practice is for everyone in that we all suffer in daily life, and our intentional words and actions can influence the outcome and character of that life. The sutra is not as well known to Secular Buddhists as the more commonly quoted Kalama Sutra, often referred to as the Buddha's discourse on free inquiry, and is a relatively short scripture. Yeshe Rabgye unpacks the thirty-eight principles of the Mangala Sutra with a strong foundational exposition of the core principles of Buddhism, all the while showing how they are equally applicable to all people in this very moment. Each principle in the Mangala Sutra is accompanied by an exploration of what it means to the contemporary practitioner, with clear instructions for contemplative inquiry to discover how it may provide beneficial insights to the reader's unique experiences in life.

Throughout this book and his previous work, *The Best Way to Catch a Snake*, Yeshe Rabgye elegantly navigates the difficult waters of tradition and contemporary thought, honouring both, and making this transformative practice meaningful to all. Neither book should be simply read and accepted with the intellect, but fully absorbed and incorporated into one's daily life, creatively in each moment.

    Ted Meissner
    Founder
    Secular Buddhist Association

Introduction

WHEN I BECAME a Buddhist monk, I made a point of trying to read all of Gautama Buddha's early sutras, not because I'm a scholar or anything, but because I was finding huge discrepancies in the commentaries. I thought it prudent to go back to the nearest thing we have to Gautama Buddha's actual words. Whilst I was researching these sutras I came across the Mangala Sutra, and it seemed to switch a light on inside of me. I spent weeks reflecting on the thirty-eight principles, and came to the conclusion that this is a path we can all follow, whether we are Buddhist or not. But to what end?

Now, this is where we may all differ. When asked, many traditional Buddhists say enlightenment is the end game. However, I always find this a bit disconcerting when people offer up such a goal. If you push them a little further, they talk about going to a different place, such as nirvana, not being born again, or residing in a Buddha field in some celestial realm. It appears they think of these places of enlightenment as a paradise full of all the nice things we like, and devoid of anything we dislike. They also look upon it as something outside of ourselves. I feel these are all misunderstandings of what Gautama Buddha actually wanted us to aim for.

I believe Gautama Buddha's main point was that life is full of suffering from birth through to old age and death, and we ourselves are the main cause of this suffering (although not the only cause). In the Majjhima Nikaya he explains what he taught:

> 'One thing and one thing only do I teach, suffering and how to end suffering'.

The paths he spoke about in his teachings are a way for us to try to alleviate this suffering and live a calmer, more responsible life.

Now, before we go on, I should explain the use of the word *suffering*. In Gautama Buddha's teachings the word used is *dukkha*, which has commonly been translated as suffering. The suffering we are talking about isn't just physical pain, but also emotional torment. It includes a feeling of dissatisfaction, anxiety, anguish, unhappiness, desire, discontent, unease, a feeling of not being whole, frustration, and even depression. The list could go on, but I think you get the picture. So whenever I use the word *suffering*, I am using it as an umbrella term to cover all of the above.

I do not believe Gautama Buddha meant for us to dream of going to a different place once we die—such as nirvana, paradise or heaven—or to project all the things we like in this world onto these places. Heaven, nirvana and so forth should be looked upon as states of mind and not actual places.

A key point to remember is that Gautama Buddha never said he was enlightened. The word *enlightenment* is a mistranslation of the Sanskrit word *bodhi*, which is actually better translated as awakened.

Once Gautama Buddha was asked if he was a god, a sorcerer, a magician, an angel, or a celestial being. He answered no to all of these. He said he was awake. Being awake is very different than being enlightened. When we are awakened it is right here, right now, in this very life. It is being awake to, or having an awareness of, the way the world really is, and the impact we have on it and the people around us. It is also within us and not something we need to go searching for in the outside world.

When asked to sum up his teaching in a single word, he said, 'Awareness'. This awareness is based on our experiences and is not achieved through blindly following a teacher or some teachings. The highest authority is our own experiences. It is not enough to rely on faith or understanding Gautama Buddha's teachings intellectually. We have to experience it as he did. His teachings are all based on his own experiences and he strongly encouraged us to do the same. This fact seems to have become hidden under a mass of dogma, tradition and culture.

I see this awareness Gautama Buddha talked about as spirituality and not religion. To me religion is a belief in another person's experiences, whereas spirituality is having an awareness of your own experiences. That is quite a big difference.

His teachings took on many beliefs, rituals, ceremonies and practices once he died, and his discourses began to move from country to country. It has also taken on superstitions and old wives' tales. I think sometimes all of these trappings are masking the true meaning of Gautama Buddha's words, which were actually practical and quite simple. We have to look at his teachings with an open and critical mind. Don't be afraid of asking questions and having doubts. Both of these are healthy. Gautama Buddha said this himself in his last discourse: 'If any amongst you has any doubts as to Gautama Buddha, the teaching or the order of monks, ask me now so that afterwards you may have no cause to regret that you did not ask me while I was still with you'.

So it is important not to suppress your doubts. British philosopher Bertrand Russell stated that wise people have doubt:

> The whole problem with the world is that fools and fanatics are always so certain of themselves, and wise people so full of doubts.

Following his teachings isn't just about bowing to teachers, building statues or stupas (a moundlike structure usually containing Buddhist relics), paying someone else to do prayers for you, or even lighting butter lamps. It is about realising that you are suffering and then becoming aware of what is causing you to suffer, understanding there is a cure, and finally, working towards cutting down that suffering. All of this is carried out in this very life, and so we do not have to wait till we are dead to become awakened. Remember, Gautama Buddha advised us to work out our own liberation in this life, not to put it off or depend on others. He stated in the Mahaparanivana Sutra that:

> 'Each of you, make yourself an island, make yourself your refuge, there is no other refuge'.

The point I am trying to convey here is that what he taught was for you to look inward; as it is you who is suffering, so it is you who has to do the work to alleviate it. Do not think that simply saying prayers or financially supporting a monastery means you will have less suffering in your life. It may or may not help, but it certainly isn't the whole solution.

We do not honestly know if we have been here before or if we will come back again. However, what we do know is that we are here now, and it is now that we are suffering. So it makes sense to try our best to reduce our suffering at this time.

To me this is a win–win situation. We reduce our suffering now in this very life, and if there is a next life, we would have set ourselves up for a good rebirth. So whether you believe in rebirth or not, you will end up winning. Gautama Buddha stated this in the Apannaka Sutra:

> 'Even if one believes there is no other world, no future reward for helpful actions or punishment for harmful ones, still in this very life one can live happily, by keeping oneself free from anger, ill will and anxiety'.

I'm not a gambling man, but even I feel these odds are great.

• • •

This book is written from a secular Buddhist viewpoint, so you may ask why is a Buddhist monk, trained in traditional Buddhism, writing a secular book? It's a good question. It is because I can see that traditional religions are failing people today, especially in the West. People are not willing to just blindly believe what is written down in ancient texts or taught by so-called holy men. Claims have to be justified and proof given or people won't accept them, and quiet rightly so.

Let me give you an example of how religions, or the way they are being interpreted, are failing people. Recently I visited a village in northern India where both Muslims and Buddhists live. When I went to the shops I was told that, as I was a Buddhist, I could only go into the shops run by Buddhists. I was not allowed to visit the Muslim-run shops. So tell me, what has that got to do with religion or helping me find my way in this world? That seems to be adding to my suffering, and other people's, and not reducing it.

I believe there is much to be learned from traditional Buddhism, but you have to work through all of the superstitions, dogma and culture to find some sort of truth that is relevant today. This is what I have attempted to do here. I have taken what I have been taught in the monastery and applied it in a secular way. It is a post-traditional Buddhism, and I hope people will find this approach of some benefit.

The book is a practical guide; it was not written to be quickly read and then put on the shelf out of sight. It is for you to slowly work through each principle, see which ones are useful to you, and then implement them. It is not possible for you to change unless you do some work. We can change only what we understand. Just reading this book and expecting changes is like knocking on an open door and waiting for someone to let you in.

I feel I should be totally honest with you here. This book is not going to lead you to enlightenment, nirvana, heaven or paradise. I will leave it for others to offer you such things. What I am attempting to offer you is a life with less discontent and unease; a life that has less tension and stress; a life whereby you take responsibility for all of your actions and stop blaming others; a life in which you will have compassion for yourself, your family, friends and all the people you come into contact; a life in which you understand what drives you and how you can change what is not working. In brief, a happier life. This is my aim here.

I am not saying that the traditional, dogmatic, metaphysical side of Buddhism is wrong or doesn't work. I am just saying that this is not how I have written this book. I have written it to improve your life now, today. It is not based on any past or future lives. Only this life!

What you need to understand is that we are all in this together. I am no different than you. I am not a higher being, superhuman or even a guru. I am just a human being trying to find my way in life. What I have written about here are things that work for me. They may not work for you, but I would urge you to at least give them a try.

I have spent many years studying, questioning, meditating and implementing Gautama Buddha's teachings, and so this book is based on my experiences, which I hope resonate with you. However, I understand that not everyone's experiences are the same. How can they be? My experiences have very little in common with a person brought up in poverty in Africa. But the suffering Gautama Buddha spoke about is universal, so try out the advice in each of the principles and see if they work for you. As I have stated, I am not offering miracles, just hard work with, I hope, a better life at the end.

If a teacher or a so-called guru offers you enlightenment, tells you he has all the answers, claims his way is the best and quickest way to nirvana and says you have to follow his every word and not question him, I would suggest you be very sceptical, or at the very least ask for proof of his seemingly outlandish claims.

Whether you are a traditional Buddhist or more secular; whether you are religious or non-religious, or whether you follow a different religion than Buddhism, I believe you can benefit from following the meandering path in this book. This is not a boastful claim, but one built on my own experiences.

After I have described each principle given by Gautama Buddha, there will be a section where you can reflect. This will enable you to think about the advice given and to see if you already adhere to it or if you need to do some work to obtain it. If you have never reflected in this way before, I have written the best way to approach this type of reflection in the next chapter.

I have also written about starting a daily review session. This is extremely important for you to get the best out of this book (and your life). I will also explain how to do this review in the next chapter.

I wish you well along this meandering path, but remember, we are humans and so we make mistakes. Some days you will feel you are on the path, and other days you may feel you have strayed a bit. Don't berate yourself; just resolve to do better tomorrow.

1
Truth is Found in Stillness

THE MANGALA SUTRA has thirty-eight principles. I believe if these principles are going to be of any use to you, it is important for you to do the following:

read—understand—reflect—implement

The reflection stage of this is extremely important. If you just read and understand these principles, it will mean you know them intellectually. That is only knowledge. However, if you reflect on them, they will become wisdom and much easier for you to implement. Wisdom here means that they become a part of your life; the very core of who you are and how you think and act. There is a difference between knowledge and wisdom. Knowledge has to do with words, concepts and theories, whereas wisdom is beyond concepts and theories. It is something you feel inside. To put it a simpler way, knowledge helps you make a living, but wisdom helps you make a life.

Reflecting is a way for us to examine ourselves, to gain insight into our experience of life. Everyone's reality is different and stems from his or her own mind. To be able to reflect, our mind has to be calm, stable and focused. It is impossible to see into a bucket of muddy water when it has been stirred up. But if you leave the water to settle, the mud will fall to the bottom and the water will become clearer. The same happens with our mind. If it is agitated, you will not be able to gain any insight; but if it is calm, stable and focused, you will be able to gain the insight you require.

To make your mind calm and stable, you will need to do some calm-abiding meditation practice before you reflect on the principles. We are all different, so I have described two types of calm-abiding techniques here. Try them out and see which one is best for you. If you already have a calm-abiding practice that works, stick with it. No need to change just for the sake of change.

Breathing Meditation

1. Find a quiet place where you will not be disturbed. It is good to have a special room or part of a room put aside for meditation. You may wish to burn incense or a candle to set the scene, but this is not compulsory, it is just something some people find helpful.
2. Choose a time when no one will interrupt you. Most people say first thing in the morning and last thing at night works best, but again, find what works best for you. It is important not to meditate straight after a meal. This may lead to you falling asleep, and

sleeping is not meditation. We are looking for some kind of awareness, and there is no awareness in sleep.
3. Turn off your mobile. Don't just put it on silent. Actually switch it off. Don't worry, nothing bad will happen!
4. Sit on a cushion with your legs crossed and your back straight, but not rigid. Rest your hands in your lap, palms up.
5. If you are unable to sit on the floor, a chair without armrests will do. Again, keep your back straight, but this time make sure your feet are planted firmly on the ground and your hands are resting in your lap. Whether you are on a chair or on the floor, it is important that you are steady and comfortable. This will help stop any swaying or discomfort during the meditation.
6. Gently close your eyes. Some teachers say your eyes should be slightly open, but I have always found that distracting. If something moves slightly in my line of vision, I lose my focus. Again, it is up to you to find what works best.
7. Sit in this position for a few minutes, taking deep breaths. This is to relax you, so you are present in the moment and not thinking about the past or the future. Breathe in fully and hold it for a second or two. Now completely expel the air, and wait a second or two before taking another deep breath. Do this ten times, i.e., ten in breaths and ten out breaths.
8. Once you are relaxed—not too much, as I don't want you to fall asleep—you are ready to meditate. Be sure your back is still straight and your eyes are

lightly closed. Now smile. Not a big cheesy grin, but a slight smile. Just turn up the corners of your mouth. No, I haven't gone mad; this will help ease any tension you may still have and put you in a calmer frame of mind. Don't be shy, try it. Now become aware of your breath going in and coming out. Place your awareness on your nostrils. You do not have to follow the breath all the way. Just be aware of where it touches the nostrils. Do not focus too hard, just become aware of it. Remember, we are doing mindfulness of the breath and not concentration on the breath. (There is a big difference between these two. Mindfulness is having just an awareness of the breath going in and out, which causes no tension. However, when we concentrate too hard, it causes tension and we do not totally become calm—which is the whole point of what we are doing here.) So breathe in and mentally count one—then breathe out. Don't force the breath, let it come naturally. Then breathe in and count two—breathe out. Breathe in and count three—breathe out. Do this up to the count of ten.

9. After the first ten, change from counting the in breath and start counting the out breath. Breathe in and then breathe out and count one. Breathe in—breathe out and count two. Again, do this up to the count of ten.

10. From then on just be aware of your breaths going in and out, don't count them. If we carry on counting it may turn into just a counting exercise and we will lose our awareness of the breath.

11. You will almost certainly have thoughts pop up between your breaths. Don't worry, it happens to us all. Do not engage the thoughts, just let them be, smile again and bring your awareness back to your breath. At first you will have many thoughts popping up all over the place, but as you get more experienced, the thoughts will become fewer. It is important to remember that we are letting the thoughts be and not trying to suppress or control them.

12. You are now ready to start your reflection. I suggest you do not alter your posture and still keep your eyes lightly closed. Think of the reflection I set for you. See what thoughts, feelings and emotions arise (people tend to get emotions and feelings confused, and this is understandable because they are similar in nature. However, an emotion is a mental state, whereas, a feeling means anything that can be experienced via our sensory organs.) Don't dismiss these, as this is what we need to work with. These will give us an insight into the depths of our mind, and help us understand what makes our reality. Stay focused on the reflection and try to really work through the principle. If bad or hurtful thoughts, feelings and emotions arise, just bring your awareness back to the breath for a time. Do not upset yourself as this is supposed to be an awakening experience and not punishment.

13. Once you have finished your reflecting, sit quietly for a few minutes, and once you are ready, slowly open your eyes. Do not jump straight up. Slowly introduce yourself back into the world.

Body Scan Meditation

1. Follow points 1 to 7 from the Breathing Meditation.
2. Once you are relaxed, you are ready to meditate. Once again, be sure your back is straight and your eyes are lightly closed. Now smile. Remember, not a big cheesy grin, but just a slight smile. Now start your body scan.
3. Start with the back of your head. Focus your full attention on this area, but don't concentrate too much or you will create more tension. Feel the back of the head. Is there any tension there? If so, release it. If not, then just be aware of how that area feels. Stay about only ten seconds or so on each area or you could start to get fixated on a certain part of your body.
4. Now move on to the top of your head and do the same procedure. Remember, place your attention there for around ten seconds.
5. Go through the rest of your body in this order: face, neck and shoulders (this is where most people hold their tension), chest, arms, hands, fingers, back, lower back, backside, thighs, knees, shins, feet and, finally, toes.
6. You should now feel totally relaxed and tension free. If you are still holding some tension, redo the scan. When you are ready, start your reflection as set out in point 12 of the Breathing Meditation.
7. Remember, once you have finished your reflecting, just sit quietly for a few minutes, and move only when you feel ready. Stand up slowly so you can introduce

yourself back into the world in a calm and peaceful way.

It may seem at first that meditation is difficult. This is because our minds are restless and always want to be entertained, just like children. So when we try to slow them down and keep them still, they fight back and throw all sorts of thoughts, feelings and emotions at us. Persevere, as it will get easier. Remember, the path is meandering and so you are going to have good and less good sessions. Don't get discouraged by the less good times, and don't get carried away by the good times—just stay focused. Every session and every moment in meditation is never the same—you can't step into the same river twice—so don't try to re-create what has gone before.

It is very important to put in the effort. Athletes and musicians have to put in the effort to reach the height of their game, and you have to do the same. You can't meditate once a week for a few minutes and expect results. You should try and meditate at least once a day, but of course, twice would be better.

Try this—commit to doing two ten-minute meditation sessions a day for twenty-one days. You will really feel a difference, and after these twenty-one days, I believe, you will want to carry on.

Some days are going to be easier than others, but don't make excuses for missing a session. Remember, you are only cheating yourself! Having said that, meditation is not supposed to be a chore or a punishment. Look upon it as a positive thing, and remember that the work you are doing with your mind can be done only by you. No one else can work on your mind but you.

If you are finding it too difficult to do on your own, I suggest you join a meditation group. It is always easier to meditate in a group at first, and you will get the added bonus of a skilled teacher guiding you through the difficult times.

• • •

Once you have read, understood, reflected on and started to implement the principles, a very good tool to check your progress along the meandering path—and to understand your thoughts, feelings and emotions—is to do a daily review. This will also help you develop mindfulness throughout the day.

Many years ago when I first moved to India, I went to see a Buddhist teacher to get a personal instruction. We chatted for around thirty minutes, and then he told me at the end of each day to sit quietly and review all my actions, thoughts, feelings and emotions for that day. Think of what was good and what was not good: the things that were less good I should make a conscious effort to avoid doing again, and the good things I should make a conscious effort to continue doing. I wasn't very impressed at first as I was looking for something a bit more magical, but after carrying out the instructions for a few days, I started to get the point. What he was asking me to do was take responsibility for my actions and understand what is driving me to make those actions. I think it was the one single thing that has helped me the most in my life, and I am forever indebted to this teacher.

Gautama Buddha gave his son, Rahula, similar advice in the Ambalatthika Rahulovada Sutra. He asked him what a mirror is for, and his son answered for reflecting. Gautama Buddha then states:

> 'In the same way, Rahula, bodily action should be done with reflection and consideration; verbal action should be done with reflection and consideration; mental action should be done with reflection and consideration.
>
> 'Purify bodily action through repeated consideration and review; purify verbal action through repeated consideration and review; purify mental action through repeated consideration and review'.

Gautama Buddha was talking about reviewing our actions of body, speech and mind, and this is what I am also suggesting here. Do a daily review before you go to bed. There is no need to go through a calm-abiding meditation, as this is different than the reflection section; but if you find it easier to meditate beforehand, feel free to do so.

Find a quiet place to sit and work through your day. You do not have to be sitting on the floor, but from my experience, I think it is better to be sitting in an upright position so you do not fall asleep.

So that you are present in the moment, do the three breath-calming techniques. This entails taking three deep breaths. As you are breathing in, mentally count to five, hold the breath for a second or two, and then push your breath out, again counting to five. When you breathe in, take a really deep breath that goes right down inside, and when you breathe out, be sure you expel all of the air inside you. If you do this three times you will feel relaxed, focused and present in the moment. (I have also found this technique extremely useful when I feel anger or some other negative emotion arising. It helps me to calm down and let the negative emotion be, which means I do not engage with it or repress it.)

Now start to look at your actions of body, speech and mind from that day. Look at the good and not-so-good situations. Be honest with yourself, or there will be very little benefit. Use the principles in this book as a framework, but you can do this review any time and do not need to wait till you have read a principle. You should try and get into a habit of reviewing your thoughts, feelings and emotions on a daily basis, even after you have finished this book. In fact, especially after you have finished this book, because you need to carry on the good work you have started by following the principles laid out in the rest of the chapters.

We go through life at such breakneck speed and never take time to stop and examine our thoughts, feelings and emotions. We just seem to accept them. We say things like, 'I have always been an angry person', 'I've been jealous since I was a kid', or 'I hate this and love that' —we never look at why that is or try to change it. This daily review will help you stop and look at what is driving these emotions and feelings. It will help you to act instead of react to situations.

If we do stop and look, we may be surprised at what is driving us. It could be a throwback from your childhood and, because you are now an adult, it has become an outdated way to be. So use this review session as a mechanism for change, but remember what I said earlier: change can come only through understanding. The review session is a way for us to understand our inner workings.

We may find thoughts, feelings and emotions come up that are not helpful, and not a responsible way for us to be acting. Don't panic; just acknowledge them, let them know you have registered them, and then let them be. You do not have to follow or adopt everything that comes up. This is where you can make changes and develop skills that will counteract your negative way of acting. See what works and what doesn't. Adopt what works and leave what doesn't. A note of warning: do not suppress the unhelpful thoughts, feelings and emotions. This is not going to help you in the long run.

When you look back and find a situation in which you didn't act in a helpful way, look at what thoughts, feelings and emotions surrounded that act. What drove you to act in such a way? Was it jealousy, pride, fear, anger, pleasure or pain? Once you know the driving force, you can begin to rehearse a better way to act. This will be your antidote should the situation arise again. A word of warning here: be sure you are not replacing one negative way of acting with another. We are not rearranging the furniture here; we are having a clear out, exchanging our old furniture for new.

After some time you will become more skilled at spotting unhelpful thoughts, feelings and emotions as they arise. You will then be able to implement the antidote before you do an unhelpful act. But this takes time, so for now use the daily review to look back over the day and see what worked well and what didn't. What we are trying to do is embrace the things that worked and leave the things that didn't work by replacing them with helpful ones.

Another word of warning: do not identify with the negative thoughts, feelings and emotions. Don't think, 'I am unhappy' or 'I am depressed'. Think along the lines of, 'There is unhappiness' or 'There is depression'. If we personalise what is going on, it will be extremely hard for us to let it be or try another strategy.

Let's now talk a little about the power of our thoughts. It is important for us to understand that our thoughts drive our actions; it is not the other way around. Gautama Buddha said:

> 'We are what we think. All that we are arises with our thoughts. With our thoughts, we make the world'.

This is an extremely important point, because if we believe the world is created by some outside force, we will never be able to change. That is also the case if we believe in destiny. If we believe things are predestined, there will be no need for us to try to change, because our future is already mapped out by some higher being or outside force. This is why Gautama Buddha stated that whatever arises comes from our thoughts. Take a few minutes to reflect on this point, as a full understanding of this will help you make changes in your life.

The following quote is attributed to Gautama Buddha, and aptly sums up how powerful our thoughts are and what stems from them:

> 'The thought manifests as the word; The word manifests as the deed; The deed develops into habit; And habit hardens into character. So watch the thought and its ways with care, and let it spring from love born out of concern for all beings'.

So if we want change, we must look at our thoughts and the feelings, emotions and actions that stem from them.

Do not underestimate the power of your mind. The mind is extremely good at gathering, storing and analysing information. It then uses this information at a later date. This means the mind is conditioned by the past, and so it will always try to re-create what it knows and is familiar with, even if it is painful. This means we are always operating from outdated concepts and beliefs that make our lives an elaborate illusion.

Because the mind is conditioned, it follows that our thoughts stem from old habits, training and social conditioning. We actually believe we are creating new possibilities, but when we take the time to watch our thoughts, we find we are just recycling old patterns that have been learned from teachers, religions, parents, friends, society and so on. The thought may have passed its sell-by date and is no longer serving us, but if we don't stop and look, we will not be able to change the harmful ones or reinforce the helpful ones. We will just continue to blindly follow them. This is one reason why people who have an addiction keep repeating their destructive behaviour. Their mind is conditioned and it just re-creates what is familiar and, for them, safe. So I cannot express just how important being aware of your thoughts is.

In the introduction I mentioned awareness, and this is where we can start to become aware of the thoughts that are colouring our world. Remember, awareness means to wake up from our sleep and become aware of how the world really is. We tend to tell ourselves stories, which we believe to be true, so we have to look past those and investigate our experiences. Why do we think like we do?

Why do we say things? Why do we act in a certain way? Why do we hate this, but love that? These are all questions we have to grapple with at our review session. Only then can we become aware of what drives us.

It seems we do not give much importance to our thoughts. We tend to attach the most importance to physical actions, less to speech, and least of all to our mental actions. Beating a person seems to us a more serious action than speaking to him insultingly, and both seem more serious than the ill will we have toward that person.

This is the wrong way round. The most important is our thoughts because, as I have stated above, our actions spring from them. It doesn't matter how many mantras you recite; how many prostrations you do; where you go on a pilgrimage; what so-called higher practice you follow; what language you chant your prayers in; or who your teacher is—if you haven't become fully aware of your thoughts, these practices are not going to give you the change you desire. That change can come about only when we become aware of what thoughts are arising, and how we deal with these thoughts.

Let's look at an example. You have spent the last hour chanting prayers and you are feeling good about yourself. However, once you get outside, someone cuts you off in your car and you get angry. You start ranting and raving at this person—so what use are your prayers now? Your prayers have not given you an insight into your mind or given you an antidote to your anger. I am not saying these practices are a waste of time, because they're not. But if you do not investigate your mind, the practices are not going to work.

So this is why it is important for us to become aware of our thoughts. In this way we can start to weed out the negative ones and plant positive ones. It isn't easy because our mind is lazy and will constantly try to return to its default mode, which it feels comfortable with. We do our best to seek out company and entertainment to keep us from facing up to life. However, we have to persevere and bring it out of its comfort zone. This can sometimes be painful, but stick with it as it is going to be worth it in the end.

As it can be painful sometimes, you should be gentle with yourself. This review is here to help you, so don't push yourself too hard. Work slowly, as you will not be able to change everything at once. The things that drive us have built up over the years, in fact since the moment we were born, so they are not going to loosen their grip instantly. Look upon yourself as a tree that is deeply rooted in the ground and be patient. Training the mind is similar to potty training a baby. You constantly have to keep showing it a better way to act.

• • •

When we do our meditation/reflection practice and daily review, I am sorry to say it will not all be clear sailing. There are five things that Gautama Buddha taught that will interfere with, obstruct and impede our progress. These are called the five hindrances and they are five negative mental states. In the Mahatanhasankhaya Sutra, Gautama Buddha described the five hindrances in this way:

> '...imperfections of awareness that weaken discernment...'

The five are sensual desires, ill will, apathy and laziness, anxiousness and doubt. In Buddhism it is stated that:

> 'All those that have been freed from delusion have done so by removing the five hindrances that defile the mind and weaken understanding'.

Let's look at these hindrances individually.

Sensual desire is straightforward. They are desires of the senses. This hindrance is activated when our senses come into contact with sense objects, such as eye to form, ear to sound, nose to smell, tongue to taste, body to tangibles and mind to thoughts. Every time we point our concentration at our practice, this hindrance may pop up and distract us. We get stupefied by these sense objects, and we start to crave them and feel attachment towards them.

The antidote to this is to think about the impermanence of objects. This topic will be fully looked at in principle 36, so for now I will just give you an outline.

If things are compounded, that is to say, made up of two or more things, they are by their very nature impermanent.

The parts come together, last for a period of time and then change/die. You can clearly see this in your friends and family, your belongings and even your body.

Ill will is to have angry and hateful thoughts towards someone, though it is also possible to have ill will towards a situation or even yourself. It can make you burn inside, and you are unable to concentrate on anything else but your hatred. It is usually driven by resentment, jealousy, pride or anger.

This is an extremely powerful hindrance, and the antidote is to reflect on compassion towards others. The reason we have ill will is because we see other people as different than us, as outside of us. We do not see the interconnectedness of life. If during your daily review you think about what you want and don't want out of life, you will see you are striving to be happy and trying not to suffer. You are not alone. Everyone is exactly the same, even animals. So if we see that others are no different than ourselves, we will build compassion towards them, or at the very least we will be empathic towards them. This is how we stop ill will.

Apathy and laziness make our mind numb so it is virtually impossible for us to concentrate. The first one makes it really difficult for you to arouse any interest; the second makes you lethargic and sleepy. They both make it very hard for you to do any practice
.
The antidote for both of these is quite simple. You could open a window and let some air in, go for a walk, splash water in your face, have a break or a cup of tea. It is

up to you how you do it, but you have to wake yourself up and become more alert.

Anxiousness is when we are feeling tense and irritable. It could be that we are stressed from work or the journey home. You may have money problems, be worried about the future or your mind is just overloaded. This hindrance makes you overexcited and emotionally troubled. You are not able to concentrate on anything for any length of time. This is because you are not in the present moment. Your thoughts are either in the past or the future.

The antidote, which will bring you into the present moment, is to do the breathing or body scan meditations I mentioned above, or, at the very least, the three breath-calming techniques. This will relax you and put you in a better frame of mind to continue.

Doubt is when we have a lack of confidence. It could be we don't understand what we should be doing, or we don't trust that it works or we think we are not doing it correctly. All of these make us wonder if what we are doing is benefiting us.

The most simple and effective way to clear up doubt is to ask questions, read books or surf the Internet for answers (be careful here as the net is full of misinformation). In certain forms of traditional Buddhism, doubt is looked upon as a very unhelpful thing. You are told to just believe your teachers and not question what they say. I find that extremely unhelpful. I have always asked lots of questions if I do not understand something, and it has always cleared away my doubt.

I feel that if you blindly follow something or someone, you are setting yourself up for trouble later on. Doubt doesn't disappear just because a teacher has told you not to ask questions. In fact, it will just stay there and fester, waiting for a chance to pop up later and make you have even more doubt.

Sometimes people do not like to ask their teachers questions because they feel the question may be stupid. I would say that it is more stupid not to ask the question, as you will be carrying the doubt around with you for a long time.

These are the five hindrances. We can use these five in our daily review as instruments for change. Look at them and see which ones apply more to you than others. Grade them from one to five, one being most important for you to change and five least important. Work on the most important first. Set yourself goals and boundaries, and then work towards them. Check back from time to time to note your progress.

If you are consumed by desires, look at what is making you dissatisfied. Why are you always wanting new things? Is it peer pressure, unhappiness with your life, greed or are you a shopaholic? It is only when we have gotten to the root of these desires that we can start to change.

If it is ill will that affects you most, see what causes you to feel that way. See how it is affecting your life and the lives of others around you. Are you jealous of someone, carrying around anger or do you have too much pride? If you know what causes your ill will, you will be able to cut it off at the root.

What makes you lazy and disinterested? Is it boredom, are you unwell, not understanding what you are supposed to be doing or are you just not seeing any benefit from the things you do? Give it a lot of thought and get right into the causes of this laziness.

If you are anxious about everything, find out why. Is it stress, illness, work, lack of money, loneliness or depression? Dig deep and find what makes you anxious. Then you can start to change.

Look at the doubt you carry around with you. Find out where the doubt is in your life. See how it is affecting your life and holding you back. Don't see your doubt as a negative thing. See it as a way for you to change.

If we set ourselves goals like this, we will be able to start letting the hindrances be and change our lives for the better. We have to understand that the hindrances are mental states and, as such, stem from our mind. So it is no good to blame anyone else for you having a hindrance. You may think it is another person's fault that you have ill will, work is making you anxious or it's the teacher's fault that you have doubt. All of these are wrong. It is your mind that is bringing up the hindrance, and so it is only you that can deal with it.

2
It's All in the Tea Leaves

FOR CENTURIES PEOPLE have been indulging in superstitions, lucky charms, omens, divinations and fortune-telling. They have used these things to help them make decisions and keep them from taking responsibility for their own actions. Some cultures still place a lot of importance on such things. However, if you look carefully, you can see these things stem from ignorance and fear. They certainly are not a reliable way to help you navigate through life.

In Gautama Buddha's day you could put superstitions and omens down to a lack of education, but I am not sure what the reasoning is behind them in today's society. You still see people touching wood or keeping their fingers crossed to bring them good luck. Others wear a rabbit's foot for the same reason—though I think it is not very lucky for the rabbit. They don't put new shoes on a table, walk under ladders or open umbrellas in the house just in case it brings them bad luck. People become visibly scared if they break a mirror or spill salt, and don't even mention Friday the thirteenth.

In Tibetan culture it is inauspicious to start a journey on a Saturday. So people pack their things on Friday and leave the house as though they are starting their journey. But they only take their bag to a friend's house and then return home. On Saturday they collect their bag and start their journey, believing they have tricked the superstition. It is clear that this type of ignorance only creates a vicious cycle where superstitions are used to cheat other superstitions.

The list of superstitions and omens is endless, but they have one thing in common: they are totally irrational and based on fear and ignorance.

People go to fortune-tellers, psychics and gurus for divinations so they can shirk their responsibilities and get someone else to make an important decision for them. But if these people can see into the future, it would mean our lives are predetermined. That would in turn mean we could never improve our lives, as things have already been decided for us. Thankfully, this is not the case, and people who say they can see into the future are just playing on people's ignorance and fears. You may say there is no harm done, but I beg to differ. I heard of a man who was seriously ill going to a guru for a divination. He was told not to have an operation but to do some prayers instead. This person died needlessly, and painfully, because if he had had the operation, he more than likely would have survived.

There is a famous, or infamous, psychic in America, and when I was writing this book she hit the headlines, and not in a positive way. Ten years ago a young girl went missing, and the psychic told the family she was dead and they would see her again only in heaven. It transpired that the girl wasn't dead but was being held captive for all those years. The family say the mother died of a broken heart after the psychic reading.

These two stories show just how harmful this type of trickery can be. I believe these people are acting irresponsibly and fraudulently.

Many go to holy people for blessings, believing that if they are touched on their head or they touch the feet of a guru, their lives will be OK. They also may wear something around their necks, hoping it will protect them from danger. They also go to long-life ceremonies thinking that they will live a long time, even though they do not do anything to change their actions or life-style. Again, these things are just superstitions, and without you exploring your thoughts and changing your actions of body, speech and mind, you will not be able to change your life.

Gautama Buddha called all of these practices 'low art', and on many occasions he stated that such things are of no use as we have to take responsibility for our own lives.

In the Anguttara Nikaya, Gautama Buddha stated that this is how responsible people act:

> 'They do not get carried away by superstition; they believe in deeds, aspiring to results from their own deeds through their own effort in a rational way; they are not excited by wildly rumoured superstition, talismans, omens or lucky charms; they do not aspire to results from praying for miracles'.

There is a story about a Brahman who was an expert in predictions drawn from cloth. He held a superstition that once a piece of cloth, no matter how new or expensive, was bitten by a rat, it would bring you bad luck.

On one occasion he discarded a piece of his expensive cloth in a local cemetery because he believed it had been bitten by a rat and would now bring him only bad fortune. Later on he heard that Gautama Buddha had picked up the cloth and was using it. He ran as fast as he could to find Gautama Buddha and warn him about the bad luck that was going to come his way if he didn't throw the cloth away. However, once the Brahman found him, he was dissuaded from this irrational superstition and shown that only he himself could bring good or bad circumstances into his life.

Gautama Buddha did not believe in luck, fate or chance. He taught that whatever happens does so because of a cause or causes. If you want to pass your exams, you have to study hard and put in a lot of effort. So there is a clear connection between passing the exam and study. It is of no use praying to a god, chanting a mantra or wearing some kind of lucky charm to pass your exam as there is no connection between these things.

So what did Gautama Buddha believe? He believed in individual responsibility, rational thought and social obligations rather than unhealthy fears and irrational superstitions. This point was made very clear in the Mangala Sutra. In this discourse, Gautama Buddha was asked what the most auspicious omens were and which ones should be followed. He didn't directly answer the question, but instead gave guidelines of how we can make our own lives auspicious without relying on outside omens. He spoke about thirty-eight principles that, if lived by, would bring us true protection.

These thirty-eight principles gradually lead you on a journey that will see you reforming yourself and turning into a responsible person within society. It is a practical guide that will help you find happiness and ease your suffering. It not only shows you what you need to do, but it also shows you the inevitable obstacles you will encounter whilst you travel along the path. Remember, the path is not a straight run from A to B. You will have good and bad days. I have called this book *Life's Meandering Path* because that is exactly how it is going to be. There will be days where you will make good progress, and others that will take you back a step or two. The important thing is to carry on along this meandering path and not become disillusioned or be distracted by the bad days.

The thirty-eight principles will lead you through individual discipline, family obligations, social responsibility, and, finally, to personal development. In a nutshell: it is a guide to life.

The excellent thing about this sutra is that it is firmly planted on earth. It is not metaphysical, and you are not required to pray to or believe in any superior beings or mythical characters. It is written for ordinary people and so has universal appeal. It can be followed by anyone as it is not religious and does not involve any ritual practices or ceremonies. You do not need to buy anything or even call yourself a Buddhist. It truly is a breath of fresh air.

The thirty-eight principles are divided into five categories:

A) Foundation Principles
    1—Avoid people exerting a negative influence
    2—Associate with people who exert a positive influence
    3—Show respect to those who have earned it
    4—Live in a suitable location
    5—To have done good deeds in your past
    6—Be on a suitable path

B) Supporting Principles
    7—Have good learning skills

8—Have practical skills
9—Follow a code of discipline
10—Practice appropriate speech
11—Support your parents or guardians
12—Take care of your spouse and children
13—Have an appropriate livelihood and balanced life-style

C) Social Principles
14—Be charitable
15—Practice virtuous actions
16—Help your friends and relatives
17—Be blameless in one's own conduct
18—Refrain from harmful acts
19—Exert great effort
20—Refrain from intoxicants
21—Be diligent in your practice

D) Individual Principles
22—Venerate those worthy of it
23—Be humble
24—Be content
25—Be grateful
26—Receive teachings at a favourable time
27—Have patience
28—Giving and listening to advice
29—Have a teacher
30—Discuss the teaching

E) Refining Principles
31—Practice self-restraint

32—Understand the four truths
33—Follow the eightfold path
34—Work towards freedom from suffering
35—Be unaffected by worldly conditions
36—Understand impermanence and nonself
37—Free yourself from defilements
38—Achieve lasting peace and true happiness

The next chapter contains the full text of the Mangala Sutra, and in the following chapters I will discuss all of the thirty-eight principles individually.

• • •

By oneself is evil done;
by oneself is one defiled.
By oneself is evil left undone;
by oneself is one made pure.
Purity and impurity depend on oneself;
no one can purify another.

You yourself must strive;
Gautama Buddha only points the way.
Those meditative people who tread the path are released from the bonds of unhelpful emotions.

Before we set out on this journey, I wanted to share these verses (Nos. 165 and 276) from the *Dhammapada* (an anthology of 423 verses from Gautama Buddha) and reiterate a point I was making in the introduction. These verses make it clear that if you want purity, you have to do it yourself. If you want to be a good and responsible person, you have to do it yourself. If you want to ease your suffering or change something about yourself—such as destructive emotions like anger, jealousy, pride and so on—you have to do it yourself. This is the common theme running through all of Gautama Buddha's teachings. He cannot change you, nor can anyone else. You have to do it yourself. You are the one that has to walk this meandering path of thirty-eight principles. Nobody can walk it for you! So get your hiking boots on and set off along this rewarding path.

3
The Mangala Sutra

Thus have I heard:

Once Gautama Buddha was staying near Savatthi in the Jetavana monastery, and late one night a deity (a supernatural figure) appeared to him. The deity showed respect to Gautama Buddha and then said to him:

Many different types of people
have contemplated on auspicious signs
hoping for good things to happen to them.
Please tell us the most auspicious signs.

(Gautama Buddha then said the following)

Avoid people exerting a negative influence and
only associate with people exerting a positive influence.
Show respect to those who have earned it.
This is the most auspicious practice.

Live in a suitable location.
Have done good deeds in your past.
Set yourself on a suitable path.
This is the most auspicious practice.

Have good learning and practical skills.
Follow a code of discipline
and practice appropriate speech.
This is the most auspicious practice.

Support your parents or guardians
and take care of your spouse and children.
Have an appropriate and balanced livelihood.
This is the most auspicious practice.

Be charitable and practice virtuous actions.
Help your friends and relatives,
be blameless in one's own conduct.
This is the most auspicious practice.

Refrain from harmful acts with great effort.
Refrain from intoxicants
and be diligent in your practice.
This is the most auspicious practice.

Venerate those worthy of it.
Be humble, content and grateful.
Embrace Gautama Buddha's teachings at the right time.
This is the most auspicious practice.

Have patience and learn how to give and listen to advice.
Have a teacher and discuss the teaching.
This is the most auspicious practice.

Practice self-restraint and understand the four truths.
Follow the eightfold path,
and work towards freedom from suffering.
This is the most auspicious practice.

Be unaffected by worldly conditions and understand
impermanence and nonself.
Free yourself from defilements.
Achieve lasting peace and true happiness.
This is the most auspicious practice.

Those who perform these thirty-eight deeds
will be unconquered
and find true and lasting happiness.
These genuinely are the most auspicious practices.

• • •

This is my own interpretation of the Mangala Sutra and not a direct translation. I know that this sutra is chanted in several countries, but I do not think that is the point of the sutra, and so I have written it as a set of principles we should commit to following.

4
Foundation Principles

THESE FOUNDATION PRINCIPLES consist of the most basic but essential attributes everyone should have, or at least strive for. It does not matter if you are an innocent child or an intelligent professor, you should start your path to a better life by following these foundation principles. The following six principles will set the foundation on which you will be able to build the remaining thirty-two.

1—Avoid people exerting a negative influence

Who are these people who exert negative influences on us? They could be people who steal, kill, rape, harm others, deceive, lie, cheat and generally have no morality and no regard for anyone else. However, they could equally be our friends, family and acquaintances. None of us is perfect; we all have times when we are being negative or are consumed by the five hindrances. I know I am not a great person to be around when I feel apathetic or extremely tired.

There are times when even our best friends can bring us down. I had a wonderful friend who would do anything for me and was good fun to be around, but every now and again she would start to act superior. At these times she would talk in a disparaging way to me and everyone she came into contact with. When she was like this, I would start to feel embarrassed and have thoughts of ill will towards her. My mind would become extremely disturbed. It is clear that she was exerting a negative influence on me, and everyone around her, at these times.

In my daily review I would look back on the day and see how negative I had become, and it was because of the influence she was exerting on me.

When we are surrounded by negativity, we can start to act in a negative way. How is this so? Well, it states in the *Dhammapada:*

> 'What we are today comes from our thoughts of yesterday, our present thoughts build our life of tomorrow: our life is the creation of our mind'.

This means our actions of body and speech stem from our thoughts. So our thoughts are extremely important. If we are mixing with people who have bad thoughts and actions, these may rub off on us. If we are constantly surrounded by negative and immoral behaviour, there is a strong possibility we will end up acting like that, especially when we are young and impressionable. I know I was extremely green behind the ears at school and was led astray on a daily basis. It was because of the negative influences exerted on me by my school friends that I had my first experience of stealing, smoking and drinking alcohol. I expect I am not alone in this. That is why Gautama Buddha warned us to steer clear of negative influences.

It states in the Sigalovada Sutra:

> Bad friends, bad companions,
> Bad practices—spending time in unhelpful ways,
> by these one brings oneself to ruin...

Having said this about negative people, we must be willing to help those who find themselves in bad ways. Gautama Buddha was not saying turn your back on these people. If we can help them in some way we must, but we have to remain mindful so we are not adversely influenced by them.

Gautama Buddha put this at the top of his list of principles, which shows the importance he places on it. We should follow his lead.

Reflection—These are the points I would like you to reflect on. If you are unsure how to do this reflection, review Chapter One:

1. Think of a time when you had been led astray by someone who wasn't acting in a skilful way—it

doesn't matter if it was many years ago. How do you feel when you remember the incident?
2. Sit with this feeling for a while. I expect you are probably feeling a little embarrassed or disappointed you were taken in. Use this feeling to remind yourself not to be fooled by negative influences again.

In your daily review you can quietly look back on the day and see if you have been affected by negative influences. If you have, look at the causes and make changes. It could be as simple as not putting yourself in a certain situation, avoiding a person at certain times or it could mean not seeing someone ever again.

2—Associate with people exerting a positive influence

These people could be the very people who are exerting negative influences on you at various times. Remember, most people are not bad all the time.

People who exert positive influences on us will help us grow in morality, wisdom and social responsibility. They clearly understand their duties within society and know the difference between right and wrong. They will stay mindful of their thoughts and actions, and so will not knowingly cause harm to others. The person can be a parent, teacher, mentor, friend or just an acquaintance. The important thing is that they have a set of ethics and boundaries that you can learn from and follow. But remember that they are only human, and so will have negative lapses from time to time.

Dhammapada, verse 76, states:

> If you see an intelligent person who tells you where true treasures are to be found, who shows what is to be found, who shows what is to be avoided and administers reproofs, follow that wise person; it will certainly be better, and not worse, for those who follow this person.

It is with these people we should be associated, because they will help us understand the importance of virtuous actions and the harm caused by non virtuous actions. They will help us cultivate a charitable, compassionate, kind and helpful manner, which will assist us to move smoothly through these thirty-eight principles, so we can reduce suffering for ourselves and others.

In the Sigalovada Sutra it states:

> The mentor can be identified by four things: by deterring you from wrongdoing, guiding you towards good actions, telling you what you ought to know and showing you the path to a better life.

You should bear this in mind when you are deciding on a suitable teacher. In the Magandiya Sutra it states that if you follow a person of integrity you will hear Gautama Buddha's true teachings, and once you have heard them, you will follow and practice them.

We all make mistakes; nobody is perfect. So don't expect your mentor, teacher, parent or friend to be above reproach, because you are going to be disappointed. What is important is they think, speak and act in a good way and exert positive influences on you.

Reflection

1. Just sit and think about all the wonderful people in your life that have helped you. There are probably many.
2. Now just focus on one particular person. See how you have grown with their help and guidance, and how this person has helped mould you into the person you are today. Think to yourself that this is the type of person you have to mix with in your life.

Here is a piece from a sutra called Upakkilesa in which Gautama Buddha talks about finding a good friend and what we should do if we cannot find one. It sums up principles 1 and 2 very well.

If one can find a worthy friend,
A virtuous, steadfast companion,
Then overcome all threats of danger
And walk with him content and mindful.

But if one finds no worthy friend,
No virtuous, steadfast companion,
Then as a king leaves his conquered realm,
Walk like an elephant in the woods alone.

Better it is to walk alone,
There is no companionship with fools.
Walk alone and do no evil,
At ease like an elephant in the woods.

Our actions of today are very much influenced by the footprints of the past, so if we have had negative influences exerted upon us, this is what we would have stored up and will lead us to act in a negative way in the future. However, if we have surrounded ourselves, as much as possible, with positive influences, our future actions will be drawn from a pool of positive experiences.

3—Show respect to those who have earned it

Traditionally, the commentaries to this text say we should respect our parents, teachers, elders and employers, but I do not think it is up to me to tell you whom you should respect. Nobody knows better than you yourself who is worthy of respect in your life.

What I would say is that respect has to be earned and not given blindly to someone with a title, a position of responsibility or someone older than you. All of these things do not guarantee that a person is worthy of any respect. If someone—anyone—has been of great assistance in your life, you should show that person respect.

I believe that people who have been born with a title or have obtained a position of responsibility need to work hard at earning respect, and not believe it is their god-given right. It is a privilege to have a title, and so people should live up to the responsibilities the title gives them—here I am thinking about Rinpoches, gurus and other so-called higher beings. If they act in an undesirable way, they should not expect people to respect them. Their deeds will dictate whether they get respect.

Respect can be shown in various ways, but basically it means returning the kindness the person has shown you, talking to them politely, helping them when they need help, being considerate, showing gratitude and generally being there for them as they have been there for you.

Some people do not like to show respect to anyone. They probably overestimate their own abilities, and so find it hard to believe someone else can do something better than they can. This is just pride and something they should work on.

When we show respect to someone worthy of it, we are practicing humility, and where there is humility, there cannot be pride.

Remember this: 'Treat others with justice and respect. In the long run, how you treat others will be how they treat you'.

Reflection

1. Think of all the people in your life that have earned your respect. Feel what it is like to have such people in your life. Think how you feel giving respect to

these people. Think what it is like to be respected by someone you have helped guide. What I am trying to do here is show you what respect feels like for yourself and the person you are showing respect to.

4—Live in a suitable location

Now this may sound a bit strange at first, but just think what it would be like to live in a war-torn country or a country ruled by a dictator or corrupt government. It certainly wouldn't be easy to openly follow some of these thirty-eight principles.

I believe in this principle Gautama Buddha is talking about a place that is suitable both materially and spiritually.

When we talk about a materially suitable place, we are talking about a place that is peaceful, secure, healthy, comfortable and well maintained. It is an area where you are able to go out after dark and your neighbours are friendly and helpful, or at the very least they are not causing you any harm. It is not always possible to live exactly where we wish to because of financial constraints or the location of our workplace. However, if we feel safe and the neighbourhood is clean and tidy, this is a materially suitable location.

If your location is ravaged by floods, earthquakes, tornadoes and other such disasters; if it is a place where you are unable to speak and act in the way you would like to; if it is a place where you are not allowed to surf the net, read newspapers or watch television; or if it is a place where the threat of terrorism hangs over you day and night—then you are not in a materially suitable location.

A spiritually suitable place would be a place where you are free to follow these thirty-eight principles, free to have your chosen religion and free to express yourself spiritually. Many people in the world do not have this freedom as they are trapped by dictators and religious fanatics.

So if we live in a suitably material and spiritual place that is a blessing indeed, and is also a good foundation for us to be able to continue along this meandering path. If we do not live in such a place, we have to do the best we can by following the principles we are able to. But remember that no one outside ourselves can rule us inwardly. When we know this, we mentally become free.

Reflection

1. Think what it is like not to have freedom. What would it be like not to be able to follow your chosen path?
2. Do a review of where you live now. Is there material and spiritual freedom? If so, be grateful and count this as a blessing and do not waste this chance; you never know how long it will last.

5—To have done good deeds in your past
Some people believe in past lives and karma; others don't. So here it is up to you to decide what Gautama Buddha

meant by the past. If you believe in past lives, you can take it that way. However, if you do not believe in past lives or are not sure, you can take it to mean deeds you have done in the past in this life. It doesn't really matter as the meaning of this principle will be the same. Gautama Buddha's main argument here is that if we accept his path, we are more likely to be careful with our actions. So it is irrelevant if you believe in rebirth or not. This is my own view; it is not the view of all Buddhists. I have personally heard Dalai Lama say that we have to believe in rebirth to be a Buddhist, but as he is a reincarnate lama, you would expect him to say that. There is no right or wrong here, and I am not saying I know better than anyone else; it comes down to your own view point.

If you have done good deeds in the past, you will undoubtedly benefit in the future. If you have been kind and helped people in the past, they will be willing to help you in the future when you need it. However, if you have refused to help people in their hour of need, you cannot expect them to run and help you when you're in trouble. This is known as cause and effect. Whatever actions we do—good, bad or neutral—there will be consequences. It is as if life is an echo, and whatever we send out comes back to us.

Let me give you an example from my own life. When I lived in London, I would give up my Christmas and work for the homeless. I and the rest of the volunteers would start on Christmas Eve and work through to the day after Boxing Day. We would collect the homeless and bring them to a warehouse where we would feed them, give them medical help, counsel them, play games, cut their hair and give them new clothes. It was obviously of great benefit to them. But the effect on me was also great. I gained empathy towards needy people, gratitude for my life, a real feeling of compassion and a true sense of worth. So I benefited in the future from these actions, although this wasn't why I helped these people.

Cause and effect runs through our lives. Sometimes we can clearly see it, and other times it is not so obvious. If you kill someone and get caught, you will go to prison. That is the obvious cause and effect. However, if you tell a lie to a stranger, you may feel there has been no effect, but it plays on your mind and causes you to be tense and ill at ease—this is subtle cause and effect. You may be able to hide this subtle effect by keeping yourself busy, but if you sit down to meditate, it will reveal itself.

Dhammapada, verses 1 and 2, state:

> ...if with an impure mind a person speaks or acts, suffering follows him like the wheel that follows the foot of the ox.
>
> ...if with a pure mind a person speaks and acts, happiness follows him like his never departing shadow.

So your past actions will help shape your life now and in the future. This is not some metaphysical law; it is plain common sense. If we do only bad things and harm people all of the time, our minds are going to be agitated. This will in turn cause our thoughts to be the same, and from that our actions of body and speech will be harmful. However, if we do not break the law, we help people, and we are a responsible person in society, our minds will be calm and stable.

This is how our past actions, and the actions we are carrying out now, will help build the foundation for these thirty-eight principles.

I should mention here that Gautama Buddha wasn't trying to make us feel guilty for past actions. We have all done good and bad things in the past—more good than bad, I hope, but there is no point beating yourself up over past acts. We have to learn from our mistakes and ensure we do not repeat them. This takes constant vigilance. Keep this at the forefront of your mind: 'past acts help shape our lives today and in the future'.

To sum it up: 'as the cause is, so the effect will be. As the seed is, so the fruit will be. As the action is, so the result will be'. This is something we need to constantly reflect on.

Reflection

1. Do our past actions have a connection with our lives now? Think this point over carefully. Once you understand the connection, you will want to

do only helpful acts, so you will be building a good future for yourself.
2. Spend time reflecting on what I said earlier: 'Treat others with compassion and respect. In the long run, how you treat others will be how they treat you'.

Please note: Do not think that by only doing good deeds that nothing bad will ever happen to you. Some situations that affect us are out of our hands. We cannot change others, but we can change the way we react to them. So, of course, we are going to have good and bad times, but what acting in a good way does is make our minds calmer and more able to face the difficult times. This alone is a wonderful blessing.

6—Be on a suitable path
What is a suitable path? It is a path that is going to bring us a sense of ease and satisfaction with our lives. It is a path that will help us understand our responsibilities and show us how we are interconnected to everyone around us. It is a path that will reduce our suffering and increase our happiness.

What it isn't is a path that promises things that it cannot deliver, such as enlightenment, or a path where we feel we are right and other people's paths are wrong, or a path that gives us more pride and other negative emotions.

There are many paths we can choose to follow. The path I am showing you here is directly from Gautama

Buddha, but without any mysticism or dogma, and so isn't something I have dreamed up myself. It is a path I am teaching from my own experience, and I am able to verify it. That doesn't mean it will work for you; the only way you can find out is by trying it.

If certain principles work for you and others don't, that is fine. Use the ones that are going to bring about a positive change in you. But a note of caution here: it is not helpful to choose the easy principles and skip the difficult ones. That is like going to a wedding and only taking the food you know and like from the buffet. If we don't try new food, how will we know if it is good for us? It is the same with the principles: if we don't try the difficult principles, how will we know if they are going to bring about any changes in us?

No path is going to be clear sailing all the time. We will hit obstacles along the way, but we shouldn't be put off by this. If we want results, we have to put in the effort. If you are just reading through this book and thinking it is a good path to follow, but you don't do any reflecting, implementing and reviewing, how do you expect anything to change? If you are a sports-person and you don't put in the effort, you will not compete in the Olympics. If you are a student and you don't study, you will not pass your exams. If you are reading this book but not putting in any effort, you will not get any benefit.

The key to getting the best out of this meandering path is to read the principles, spend time reflecting on and understanding them, implement what you have learnt and then appraise your progress in a daily review session. This is a suitable path and one that is on offer here.

Reflection

1. Think about what you want out of life. Is it enlightenment, happiness or reducing your suffering? Whatever it is, you have to decide what path you are going to take to reach your goal. Take a look at this meandering path and see what you can achieve by following it. If it suits you, make a commitment to reflect on and implement these thirty-eight principles.

Once you have decided what path is right for you, whether it is this one or not, use your daily review to ensure you are getting the best out of your chosen path.

Summary

For any house to stand up it has to have a good, firm foundation. The same is true for this path. If we try to mix only with people who exert a positive influence and steer clear of people who exert a negative influence; if we show our respect to the people who guide us in a skilful way; if we live in an area that is both materially and spiritually suitable; if we have done good deeds in the past and understand the connection between our actions earlier in this life and our life now; and if we set ourselves on the right path—a path that reduces our suffering and helps us become more responsible, then we can honestly say we have built a sound foundation. This will be your springboard to the rest of the principles.

Before we move on, let's look at ways we can use these principles in our daily review sessions. Look at your friends and associates and see what thoughts, feelings and emotions come to the surface. If they are good people and encourage you to act in a responsible way and make you happy, these are positive people. However, if they are people who cause you to have negative thoughts, make you feel uncomfortable, unhappy, angry and so on, these are people you should try to avoid. When negative thoughts, feelings and emotions arise in you, I would respectfully suggest you distance yourself from these people or the particular situation you find yourself in. Remember what I said about our actions stem from our thoughts. So a person who makes you have negative thoughts may make you take negative actions.

Review where you live and see if it is peaceful and calm with a good atmosphere. If it is, it should make you feel comfortable and happy. If the area isn't good, you may feel nervous and apprehensive. You may not be able to move due to family or financial constraints, but you can certainly be aware of what emotions arise regarding your location, and you can develop skills that will help you deal with them better.

These are just some ideas to get you started. Please remember that you are working with your own thoughts, feelings and emotions (although I talk about thoughts, feelings and emotions as three separate things, they are actually all intertwined). We are all different, so there is no right or wrong set of results from the review. What we are looking for is a sense of contentment, satisfaction and happiness, and a life that is a little less stressful and crazy. But remember: if you want these results, you have to be honest with yourself and put in the effort.

5
Supporting Principles

WE HAVE NOW built our foundation, and so it is time to put in the pillars. These are the supporting principles. They are the supports the rest of the principles will be built around.

7—Have good learning skills
For us to be able to follow a path in life, we have to first learn about it. If we do not put our full effort into learning, we may misunderstand the path, which in turn may take us off in the wrong direction, and that could cause us to suffer even more.

If you are reading this book, or at a teaching, and you are not giving it your full attention, you will not be taking anything in. It will be like pouring water into an upturned glass. No matter how much water you pour, nothing is going to go inside. If you let your mind wander or you are distracted, you will not be able to retain what you have read or heard.

If you read this or hear a teaching and within a few minutes have totally forgotten it, it would be like pouring water into a glass with a hole in it. No matter how much water you pour in, nothing stays inside the glass. Pay attention so you are able to absorb and implement the teaching.

If you are reading or listening to a teaching and you have the wrong attitude—such as feeling you know better than the teacher, you don't believe what is being said or you think it will never be able to help you—it would be like pouring water into a glass with poison inside. No matter how pure the water is, once it goes inside the glass it will become poisoned.

So you should take the teachings on board with an open mind. Now, I am not saying you should suspend your critical thinking, but at least take in the teachings and reflect on them later. Do not dismiss every word as soon as it has been said just because it does not fit in with your current state of mind.

To have good learning skills and get the best out of the teachings, you should be like a glass that is upright, unbroken and clean. This way whatever you hear or read will stay inside and you will be able to understand, reflect and implement the teaching.

Reflection

1. What type of glass are you when you are studying? Be honest. Think about the different types of glasses and their drawbacks.

It may be that you are sometimes the glass with a hole in it, and at other times you are like an upturned or poisoned glass. This could be due to the five hindrances, so whenever you are not absorbing the teachings, look to see which of the hindrances is holding you back. That way you will be able to apply the antidote and get the best from the teaching.

8—Have good practical skills
Once you have learned a new skill you have to be able to implement it, or what is the point of learning the skill? This is where practical skills come in useful.

If you have started learning these thirty-eight principles, or any other path, the next step would be how you can fully understand them. For this you need a calm and steady mind—so you will need meditation skills. If our mind is not calm and steady it will be agitated, and our thoughts will be blown all over the place like a discarded bag in the wind. This is where the skill of calm-abiding meditation comes in. Once we have calmed our mind we can become more focused, and our thoughts are more likely to stay on the task at hand.

After that you need to give much thought to what you are being taught—this needs reflection skills. This is where we can focus our thoughts on one particular aspect of the path. If we are not looking deeply into what we are being taught, we could end up just blindly believing things. This is not a sound basis on which to travel down any path. What appears to be true to someone may not seem true to you. This is why we should not blindly believe anything.

Approach what you are being taught with an open but critical mind.

Once you fully understand the teaching or principle and have implemented it, you will need to check your progress—this needs daily review skills, such as sitting quietly and examining your thoughts, feelings and emotions. It is good to set yourself goals so you can see if you are reaching them or falling short. The review session is a time for you to reassess your goals and make changes if needed.

So you can see it is extremely important for you to be able to have learning and practical skills in order to move along your chosen path.

Reflection

1. Think of the skills required to follow this path or a similar path. Which of the skills do you have and which do you need to acquire? If there are skills you need to gain, I suggest you obtain those skills before you move any further along your path. If you do not, you may be missing some keys aspects of what is being taught, or you may be implementing them incorrectly.

9—Follow a code of discipline

As we do not live in a vacuum, we have to adhere to rules and regulations or else society would just break down into anarchy. We all have to have a set of morals or a code of ethical conduct to which we choose to adhere. I use the word *choose* because I believe we have to personally buy into a code of ethics. If they are imposed on us, we may not follow them wholeheartedly.

Gautama Buddha taught the five precepts as a way to keep ourselves in check. They are not a list of 'thou shalt not' commandments, but five things we should try to refrain from doing—not because we have been told not to do these things, or if we do them we will burn in hell, but because we want to do them; we see the benefit of doing them. The beauty of this code of ethics is that it is willingly undertaken by practitioners so they can work towards achieving a certain goal. The goal here is a reduction in their own suffering and in the suffering of others. So we should look upon this code as the starting point and an absolutely essential part of the path. We all need boundaries by which we can keep ourselves in check, and I feel these precepts are an excellent set of boundaries.

The precepts, sometimes known as the five faultless gifts, provide a skilful foundation for personal and social growth. Gautama Buddha was not being moralistic here; instead, he was showing us that if we want to be a responsible person within society, we have to ensure we are not harming anyone or anything. By following these five precepts we will also ensure that our conscience is clear, and this will help in our meditation/reflection practice. It is extremely difficult to meditate/reflect if our mind is full of guilt, remorse and tension.

The precepts are a set of rational and practical principles that are based on individual experience. This is an important point because if we follow this code we will experience changes within ourselves, and I hope, people around us will also see a difference in the way we act and follow our example.

When I first decided to become a Buddhist monk, I was given these five precepts and told to hold them for six months. After six months I had to return to my teacher and discuss how I got on. Only after that was I allowed to take my full vows. I found them to be easy to understand, but not so easy to keep on a daily basis. Every morning I would recite them before I got out of bed as a kind of a mental reminder. If I strayed during the day, which I invariably did, I would retake the precepts and strengthen my resolve not to break them again. It is because of having this experience that I now believe the precepts to be hugely important and a wonderful springboard to the path.

Gautama Buddha said this in the Abhisanda Sutra:

> Now, there are these five gifts, five great gifts—original, long-standing, traditional, ancient, unadulterated, unadulterated from the beginning—that are not open to suspicion, will never be open to suspicion, and are unfaulted by knowledgeable contemplatives and Brahmans.

What five?

1. To undertake the precept to refrain from harming or killing other beings.
2. To undertake the precept to refrain from taking what has not been given.
3. To undertake the precept to refrain from sexual misconduct.
4. To undertake the precept to refrain from telling lies.
5. To undertake the precept to refrain from the abusive use of intoxicating drinks and drugs.

Refrain from killing or harming other beings—this precept does not just cover killing humans; it also covers animals, big or small. I have added harming other beings as well because I believe if we harm or kill, we will have similar mental torment. I should make it clear here that I am talking about intentional and/or unnecessary killing. It is very difficult to go through life without unintentionally killing things. When we wash vegetables we are more than likely killing small insects, but this is not our intention. Our intention is to prepare the vegetables for eating, so this is not what the precept is about. Having said that, we should check the vegetables beforehand to ensure there are no insects on them.

What this precept is about is refraining from intentionally killing. We have to understand that all beings have the equal right to live and be free from suffering, so that is why we have to refrain from doing them any harm.

Once you get into the habit of killing, it is very hard to break that habit. You may see a mosquito on your arm and squash it. You do the same the next time a mosquito lands on you and the time after that. Eventually you do not even have to look; you just automatically squash it. This is when the act of killing has become a habit.

The way to prevent ourselves from killing/harming is to understand that all beings are the same as us. They want to be happy and not suffer. So if we know this, a feeling of compassion will rise in us and it will become much harder to kill/harm.

On a personal note, I would add refrain from eating meat. I know this is a personal decision and everyone has to decide for themselves just how far they take each precept, but at the very least I would ask you to consider how the animal you are going to eat was killed. There are humane and inhumane ways of killing animals. If they have been force fed, kept in a box only a bit bigger than themselves all of their lives, or if they had their throats cut and left to bleed to death, I would suggest this is inhumane. If people stopped buying products such as these, they would soon come off the market. So I would encourage you to give this point some thought next time you are buying meat.

Gautama Buddha's teachings are about not harming things, and so I find it hard to accept the fact that we are breeding animals, keeping them captive and then killing them for food. That leaves a nasty taste in my mouth. However, this is a personal choice. I would ask you to please spare the animal a thought before you pop it into your mouth.

Refrain from taking what has not been given—if we take something that has not been given or belongs to someone else, this is stealing. It may be a pen from work, sweets from a shop, or, when you were a child, taking money from your mother's purse. No matter how big or small, it is still stealing.

The first time we steal we may feel guilty and scared of being caught. However, the more you steal the less guilty and scared you are. In the end you steal just because you can and not because you need to. This is when stealing has become a habit.

We seem to have accepted certain forms of stealing and do not see it as a problem. I am talking about taking things from our place of work, such as stationery items from an office, bread or milk from a catering establishment and nails and bolts from a factory. We shouldn't fool ourselves: these things have not been given to us, and so it is stealing.

We don't like people stealing from us, so we should refrain from stealing from them. Once we get the reputation of being a thief, it will be very hard for people to trust us. So by stealing we are hurting both ourselves and others.

Refrain from sexual misconduct—this is causing harm to someone by the use of the sexual act, such as rape, sex with someone underage or sex with a married person—here the victim being the person's partner. If we physically, emotionally or mentally force someone into sex, this is causing him or her harm and is absolutely wrong. There are many people today still carrying the scars of sexual misconduct. So this precept should not be taken lightly.

I personally believe that Gautama Buddha taught the precept on sexual misconduct to help us refrain from harming someone through sex. He did not teach it to be moralistic or make people feel guilty for their sexual orientation. There is still much debate in traditional Buddhism about homosexuality, and I would like to add my thoughts here.

Is homosexuality forbidden in Buddhism? Is it sexual misconduct? Let's look at what Gautama Buddha and Tibetan Buddhism say.

Gautama Buddha stated in the third precept that laypeople should refrain from sexual misconduct. He never really elaborated on this point; he only said that a man should not have intercourse with a woman who is married or betrothed. He did of course say in the Vinaya, which are the rules for monks and nuns, that they have to take a vow of celibacy, but there is no such rule for laypeople.

So he left this precept sweet and simple. In some ways this is a good thing, as I don't think holy men and religions should concern themselves with the sexual act. However, as it is so vague, it does give others the chance to interpret it in a way that suits their world view and allows them to tag all of their prejudices onto it.

I believe that Gautama Buddha taught the five precepts to steer us away from causing harm to ourselves and others. If the sexual act is not going to cause harm it should be consensual, affectionate, loving and not break any marriage vow or commitment. It should also not be abusive, such as sex with an underage person or rape, and this includes forcing your partner into having sex. So I believe in this way a consenting, loving, homosexual act isn't in any way against Gautama Buddha's teachings.

In Tibetan Buddhism it is viewed quite differently. In fact, Dalai Lama has come out (excuse the pun) and said that from a Buddhist point of view lesbian and gay sex is considered sexual misconduct. He is not deriving this view from the discourses of Gautama Buddha, but from a fifteenth-century Tibetan scholar called Tsongkhapa. Here is a brief outline of Tsongkhapa's medieval thinking:

- He prohibits sex between two men, but not between two women.
- He prohibits masturbation as well as oral and anal sex.
- He does not allow sex for anyone during daylight hours, but allows men five orgasms during the night.
- He allows men to pay for sex from prostitutes.

- He gave a full list of what orifices and organs may and may not be used, and even what time and place people can have sex (Gautama Buddha never made these distinctions).

As you can see, Tsongkhapa heavily weighed the odds in man's favour—not surprising, as he was a man. In fact, his list seems to be aimed only at men. In Tibetan culture women should do what men want them to do. That point comes across loud and clear when married women, who are seen to belong to their husband, have no say in whether they want sex or not.

It would appear Tsongkhapa was trying to force laypeople to adhere to rules that were actually meant for monks and nuns. This way of thinking stems not from Buddhism, but is a cultural thing.

It does seem that Tsongkhapa's view is out of step with today's society, and so we have to go back to what Gautama Buddha meant by sexual misconduct. He wanted us to reflect on our acts and see if they bring harm or are helpful. So in this context, I believe if we want to know if an act constitutes sexual misconduct or not, we should ask ourselves the following questions:

- Does the act cause harm or does it bring joy?
- Is the act motivated by love and understanding?
- Would you like it if someone did it to you?
- Is there mutual consent?

If there is mutual consent between two adults, it is not abusive. If it is an expression of love, respect and loyalty, I believe it cannot be classified as sexual misconduct, irrespective of whether it is between a man and a woman, two men or two women.

As I stated earlier, I do not believe religions should get involved with people's sexuality. We cannot choose our sexual orientation, as we cannot choose our race or gender, so it is cruel to penalise someone for something out of his or her control. So in answer to the two questions posed at the beginning of this piece, I believe homosexuality should not be forbidden in Buddhism, and homosexuals should not be made to feel guilty for loving someone of the same sex. I also believe homosexuality should not be regarded as sexual misconduct if it is not causing harm and is loving and consensual.

Another aspect that should be looked at whilst considering sexual misconduct is people trafficking, that is, taking people and forcing them to enter the sex industry. It is estimated that in America around 100,000 children are forced into prostitution or pornography every year, and their average age is between twelve and fourteen years old. This clearly is not acceptable.

Refrain from telling lies—once we have lied to someone we invariably have to tell another lie to cover the first one, and then another, and another, until we have created a web of lies. It truly harms someone when they realise they have been lied to, and it will harm us when we are branded a liar.

Some say they lied so as not to hurt the other person's feelings, but have you considered how they will feel when they find out you lied? Maybe the truth is painful or difficult to say, but there are various ways of breaking it to someone. You can tell them in a kind and sympathetic way. You can support them once you have told them the truth. What you do not have to do is charge in like a bull in a china shop. However, it is kinder in the long run to tell someone the truth.

I get very upset when I have been lied to, as most people do, and so I keep this fact in mind when I am talking to others.

Refrain from the abusive use of intoxicating drinks and drugs—here I have deliberately put 'abusive use' because I believe drinking in moderation is not a problem. Nobody is saying you cannot have a glass of wine with dinner or a G&T after work. What is being said is that when we are completely inebriated, either by drink or drugs, we lose control of our body, speech and mind. This precept is quite often the cause of the previous four precepts, so is very important to adhere to.

We may be driving home under the influence and have an accident and kill someone; steal money to cover our drink or drug addiction; come out with a pack of lies because we have no control over our mouths; or have unsafe sex with someone we met in a bar, not even considering that we or they may be married or underage.

Once we have become addicted to alcohol and drugs it is extremely hard to break the habit. So it seems sensible not to put yourself in that position in the first place. We should remember the adage, 'Everything in moderation'.

• • •

If you have young children, you can teach them three of the precepts at an early age: refrain from killing, stealing and lying. This will help set them on the right track in life and give them clear boundaries they can work within. Once they are older you can introduce them to the remaining two: sexual misconduct and intoxicating drinks/drugs.

If we as adults do not at least try to refrain from these five precepts, we are not only harming others, we are also harming ourselves. Nobody wants to be associated with a killer, thief, liar, sex offender or addict. Another fact to consider is that we do not want to be killed, lied to, stolen from or sexually abused, and neither does anyone else.

So the five precepts are a good code of discipline for us to follow. However, as I stated earlier, they are a preliminary set of moral codes. They are the starting point, and by no means are they the only precepts we should follow. As we travel through these principles in this book we will be adding to these five.

Dhammapada (verses 246–247):

'One who destroys life, who speaks untruth, who takes what is not given, who goes to another man's wife or woman's husband, who gives himself/herself to drinking intoxicating liquors, he/she, even in this world, digs up his/her own root'.

Reflection

1. Think of each of these precepts in turn and consider how we may be harming someone when we do not follow them. Also, think of a time when someone has lied to you, stolen something from you or abused you when drunk or high on drugs. How did it make you feel? Sitting with this feeling should give us the encouragement to follow these precepts and not harm others.

We should reflect on the precepts not only here, but also during our daily review session. This will help us to be sure we are following the precepts at all times. However, if you have a transgression, do not berate yourself. Learn from it and try not to transgress in that way again. Remember, past mistakes should guide us and not define us.

Another useful tool is to mentally recite these precepts in the morning and throughout the day. This will help you to be mindful of them.

10—Practice appropriate speech

Gautama Buddha stated, in the Magga-vibhanga Sutra, that appropriate speech is divided into four parts:

> 'And what is appropriate speech? Refraining from lying, refraining from divisive speech, refraining from harsh speech, refraining from gossip: This is called appropriate speech'.

Refrain from lying ——this has been covered in the previous principle. I would just add here that Gautama Buddha said in a teaching he gave to his son, Rahula, called Ambalatthika-Rahulovada Sutra, that if someone feels no shame in telling a deliberate lie, there is no harmful act he will not do—a point to keep in mind.

Refrain from divisive speech—when people use divisive speech they are hell-bent on causing a severance between a person and a group of people. Divisive speech is never positive or productive. It is used only to harm.

This type of speech mainly stems from jealousy, pride or hatred. I have come across it several times in the workplace. A colleague has been promoted and some people are jealous, so they try to split the workforce. This is divisive speech.

You are jealous of your sibling, so you tell divisive stories to your parents in the hope they will favour you over your sibling. This is divisive speech.

When I lived in London, before I was a monk, I had a large group of friends who used to meet at least once a week to have some fun. One of the group members introduced to us a very attractive woman he had gone to school with. Several of the guys took a fancy to her and started to flirt. Several women took a dislike to her because of her beauty and bubbly personality. All of them started to be divisive. It eventually split the group and we stopped meeting. This is divisive speech and shows how destructive it can be.

These are just a few examples, but what is clear is that we must refrain from this type of speech because it will harm others and eventually harm ourselves. You will get a reputation for being someone who is always trying to cause trouble, and people will disassociate themselves from you.

Refrain from harsh words—these are swear words, bad language or words that are said only to cause harm. They are never useful or kind, and usually stem from anger or impatience.

If someone upsets us we can lose control and say things we do not really mean. The words are meant to hurt the other person, but usually, after we have calmed down, we regret them and the words come back to hurt us also. We must stay mindful of our speech and not allow this to happen.

Sometimes we get impatient with people when they are not doing what we want, they are doing it wrong or just differently, they are not being open and truthful or they are not doing anything and it is just us who is irritable. At these times we tend to get angry and start saying harsh words. Obviously, the way around this is to be more patient and have respect for other people's viewpoints and feelings.

When I worked in catering we had a head chef that had an awful temper (a lot of them do; I think it is partly temperament and partly the heat of the kitchen). When he was angry he would scream and shout the most horrible things. An hour or so later, once he had calmed down, he would apologise. The problem was the damage had been done. I used to think to myself 'Just how many times do I have to forgive this guy?' That of course was good practice for me to learn forgiveness and work on my own patience.

Every time you raise your voice or say harsh words, you have lost the argument. When your voice goes up, your credibility comes down.

Refrain from gossip—this type of speech stems from jealousy, hatred, aversion, ignorance or just having nothing better to do with your time. It is very destructive, cruel and can never be classed as helpful. At the time we may enjoy spreading some rumour or other, but just think how you would feel if people were saying the same things about you.

Gossip is both harmful and a waste of time. I do believe that social networking sites, such as Twitter and Facebook, encourage such unhelpful and wasteful gossip. I am not saying these sites are not of any use—I use them every day—but they can be used wrongly and end up ruining someone's reputation or career.

So the antidote to these four wrong ways of talking are: speak only truthful words, words that spread harmony and not discord, words that are kind and compassionate, words that help and not harm others.

In the Abhaya Sutra, Gautama Buddha listed three factors that determine whether a statement is worth saying:

> whether or not a statement is true
> whether or not it is beneficial
> whether or not it is pleasing to others

These three points should be considered before we open our mouths. He further stated in the Vaca Sutra that if a statement follows these rules below, it is well spoken:

> 'It is spoken at the right time. It is spoken in truth. It is spoken affectionately. It is spoken beneficially. It is spoken with a mind of goodwill'.

If we keep these in mind and follow them, we will always be in the realm of appropriate speech. We shouldn't take these four ways of inappropriate speech lightly, as words have the power to ruin lives. If you hit someone (which I am not encouraging you to do, I am speaking hypothetically), it will hurt for a short time and then disappear; but if you say harmful or cruel words to someone, the words can mentally scar and stay with them for years.

Reflection

1. Look at these four different types of speech and think of a time when they have been used against you. How did you feel? Remember, other people feel the same way, so refrain from inappropriate speech.
2. Reflect on the following words: 'the tongue like a sharp knife…kills without drawing blood'. Think about what these words mean and what implications they have for appropriate speech.

11—Support your parents or guardians
I now live in India, and over here this is a no-brainer, but in the West it isn't always so. In the East it is the children's duty to look after their parents because it is part of the culture and because people do not have pension schemes. In the West, however, many people prefer to put their parents into institutions so they can be professionally looked after in their old age. Now, I am not judging here. I am just pointing out the differences in certain cultures. It has to be said that old people are very much more independent in the West, so they may not want their children to look after them—my parents are in their eighties and are still fearlessly independent—but that doesn't excuse us from our moral duty.

Whether your parents live alone, live with you or live in an old people's home, we still have to care for them as well as we can. When you came into the world you were totally helpless. It was your parents or guardians that provided for you, kept you safe and ensured you had an education. I believe that in itself deserves our heartfelt respect.

We can show our gratitude emotionally, physically, materially and financially when it is required. Sometimes they may just want to have a chat, so make time for them. This is helping them emotionally. They may need help in and out of the bath or with some chores around the house. This is helping them physically. If there is something that will make their lives a little easier, you can buy it for them. This is helping materially. People don't usually have lots of money in old age, so you can give them money and help them out financially.

Don't think you are too busy building your own life to worry about theirs. Remember what I said about life being like an echo? The way you treat your parents may be the way you will be treated by your children in the future.

In the Sigalovada Sutra, Gautama Buddha stated this:

> 'I who was sustained by them, shall sustain them; I shall do their work for them; I shall keep up their family traditions; I shall make myself worthy of my inheritance; I shall make offerings for them when they have died'.

This may sound a little old-fashioned these days, but the sentiment is there. They helped us, and so we should help them in return.

Reflection

1. Take some time out of your busy life and think about all the things your parents or guardians have done for you. Do you think you will ever be able to repay them?

If your parents or guardians are still alive, this is a good time to call or visit them. Tell them just how much you care for them. A little bit of kindness goes a long way.

12—Take care of your spouse and children
It seems today that many people do not fulfill their basic duties to their spouse and children. Marriage is a commitment that shouldn't be taken lightly. I am not saying that all marriages should last forever; that would be unreasonable seeing that everything is impermanent and subject to change. However, whilst you are in the marriage you should be in tune with your spouse's needs and opinions. It is not just a game of love and respect, but also of compromise and forgiveness.

When children come along, it is a whole different ball game. If you bring children into the world, you have a moral duty to care for them. You must give them parental support, nurture them into a good person, educate them and teach them the difference between right and wrong. The way you treat your children will have a lasting effect on them, so be sure it is a positive one. Scientists believe that a large proportion of the concepts we carry throughout our lives are created between birth and five years old.

So you can see what an extremely important role you have in your children's upbringing.

Children mimic their parents. If they live in an abusive household where the spouse or children are mistreated, they may behave that way in the future, as these are the footprints that have been lodged in their consciousness and they may look upon them as normal.

You may not be able to shower your spouse and children with material gifts, but you can ensure them a safe and caring life, full of love and respect—that will last longer than any material object.

It is important for you to support your family in an honest way, as a dishonest way will eventually lead to trouble for you and them. A thief will eventually be caught and sent to jail, as will a drug dealer or murderer. A dishonest business will fail, and someone cheating others will soon be caught. All of these are going to bring much hardship on the family (see the next principle for more on an appropriate livelihood).

Reflection

1. Think back to your childhood. Were your parents loving towards each other or were they abusive? How did that affect you? Did your parents care for you and bring you up properly, or did they not really care about you? Again, how did that affect you? If they were good parents that cared for you,

follow their lead. If they weren't, then break that cycle and treat your spouse and children in a kind and caring way.

Reflecting in this way may bring up some painful and deep-rooted emotions. If this is the case, please seek professional help and don't try to suppress or hide your emotions.

13—Have an appropriate livelihood and balanced life-style

An appropriate livelihood is one that does not bring harm to anyone or anything. In the Vanijja Sutra, Gautama Buddha listed five professions that constitute wrong livelihoods:

> 'A lay follower should not engage in five types of business. Which five? Business in weapons, business in human beings, business in meat, business in intoxicants and business in poison'.

Traditionally these professions are dismissed out of hand, but I feel a little uncomfortable with that. I have Indian friends that have joined the army so they can provide for their parents and siblings. They didn't go into the army with the sole intention of killing people, although that may be a consequence of their action. Also, if a country didn't have an army, how long would it be before another country took it over? These days the army also does peace-keeping missions and so, in that way, is helping society.

Even though it states in the five inappropriate livelihoods that dealing in weapons is wrong, Gautama Buddha seems to have made concessions on this point. In the Chakkavatti Sihanada Sutra he told a king that an army is justified as it offers protection from internal and external threats for different classes of people in the kingdom. Also in the Seeha Senapathi Sutra, whilst talking to an army officer called Seeha, he did not advise Seeha against the army or being a commander of an army, but only advised him to discharge his duties the proper way.

He did prohibit a solider from becoming a monk whilst still in military service. The story goes that his father came to him and complained that he had insulted him by begging for meals, walking house to house along the streets in his own town. He said his relatives laughed at him and they insulted him and now he was trying to destroy his father's army. It seems that many soldiers were leaving the army to become monks because they received free food and shelter. So Gautama Buddha then promulgated a law (Vinaya) stating no soldier can become a monk.

So I think it is clear that contrary to popular belief, Gautama Buddha did not reject or prohibit soldiering as a profession. He has instead recognised the necessity of an army to provide protection to the subjects of a country.

A final word on this topic: I do not want you to think Gautama Buddha thought war and killing were good things. It states this in the *Dhammapada:*

Victory breeds hatred

The defeated live in pain,

Happily the peaceful live,

Giving up victory and defeat

Victory and defeat are two sides of the same coin of war.

So it is clear that it isn't as black and white as the list of five inappropriate livelihoods may suggest. I think what one should aim for is a profession that does not harm, is not deceitful and dishonest, one that doesn't involve trickery, treachery or any kind of fortune-telling. Gautama Buddha went into much detail regarding fortune-telling in the Samannaphala Sutra:

> ...reading marks on the limbs [e.g., palmistry]; reading omens and signs; interpreting celestial events [falling stars, comets]; interpreting dreams; reading marks on the body [e.g., phrenology]; reading marks on cloth gnawed by mice/rats; offering fire oblations, oblations from a ladle, oblations of husks, rice powder, rice grains, and oil; offering oblations from the mouth; offering blood-sacrifices; making predictions based on the fingertips; laying demons in a cemetery; placing spells on spirits; reciting house-protection charms; snake charming, poison-lore, scorpion-lore, rat-lore, bird-lore, crow-lore; fortune-telling based on visions; giving protective charms; interpreting the calls of birds and animals...[The list goes on and on] *Translated from Pali by Thanissaro Bhikkhu.*

As I mentioned in Chapter Two, any type of fortune-telling or predicting the future is a form of deceit and trickery, even if it is done by some so-called professional or religious person.

It is never right to deal in humans, such as prostitution, people trafficking, forcing children into work or teaching them to fire a weapon so they can join an illegal army. Nor is it right to make or sell illegal drugs and poisons. All of these professions bring harm to people and should be avoided.

The bottom line is that our livelihood must not bring harm to people, animals or the environment. If we stick to this we will be on the road to living a responsible life.

The second part to this is having a balanced lifestyle. This means we have to live within our means. In the Vyagghapajja Sutra, Gautama Buddha stated this:

> '…a householder knowing his income and expenses leads a balanced life, neither extravagant nor miserly, knowing that thus his income will stand in excess of his expenses, but not his expenses in excess of his income. Just as the goldsmith, or an apprentice of his, knows, on holding up a balance, that by so much it has dipped down, by so much it has tilted up; even so a householder, knowing his income and expenses leads a balanced life, neither extravagant nor miserly, knowing that thus

his income will stand in excess of his expenses, but not his expenses in excess of his income'.

As we all know, the world is going through an especially difficult time financially at the moment. This is, in part, due to people's greed. People have been seduced by material things, things they cannot afford, and so they have bought them on credit. They have been given mortgages they can never repay. They are living a life on borrowed money. Gautama Buddha's words above seem very relevant at the moment.

We are bombarded everyday with advertisements telling us we need this or that to make our lives complete. It seems our culture implicitly values desires, and we evaluate the worth of people by what they own. Corporations, hungry for profit, tell us that ladies need this cream to look young, men need to use this razor to look handsome, children need these toys to be happy, families need to drive around in a big gas-guzzling SUV—we are constantly barraged by new products. There appears to be a new smartphone, TV or electronic gadget released every week. Greed seems to be considered a virtue and not something to avoid.

A balanced life is one whereby we ensure that our income exceeds our expenditures. This is not an easy task to undertake as we look around and see that everyone has an iPhone or iPad, and that includes our peers, friends and family. The pressure is on us to conform, but we have to resist this pressure. It isn't easy and takes a lot of discipline, but it is doable.

The trick is not to be led along by our desires. We have to look at the things we need to get by and the things that are just a luxury. Buddhism would not say you shouldn't have luxuries, but it would say that we need to prevent ourselves from getting attached to them. There is no suffering in products, but there is suffering in our attachment to these products.

Obviously, we need food, clothes and a roof over our heads—these are our basic needs—but we must think carefully about other things that set off our desires. If you need the latest smartphone and have the money to cover it, then go ahead. However, if you cannot cover the cost and need to pay for it on credit, I would say leave it until you have saved enough money. I always feel happier when I have saved for something; the product then seems to mean more to me.

So check your desires, and don't let peer pressure or multibillion-dollar companies make you overspend. Live a balanced life because you will feel a lot happier and less stressed by acting in this way—no matter what the advertisers tell you.

Reflection

1. Think about your profession. Does it bring harm to someone or something? Are you deceiving people? Are you peddling false hope by fortune-telling? It's important for you to understand what impact your work is having on people, animals and the environment.

2. Think about your expenditures. Are you taken in by the latest products? Do you live within your means? If you lost your job, could you still pay all your bills? These are things we should face up to and not shy away from. A balanced life is a happy life.

Summary
To be able to support the rest of the principles, we need to have a good education, work hard and follow a basic set of ethics, such as the five precepts. We must ensure our speech is truthful, kind and will not hurt anyone. We have to support our parents, spouse and family; our work should not bring harm to another person or animal; and we should live a balanced life in which our expenditures do not exceed our income.

If you can achieve these principles, you are ready to move on to the social principles. But before you do, let's look at some ways of using the principles in a daily review session.

It may sound strange, but sometimes we don't know what is making us unhappy. We bloke it out and pretend everything is OK. So the daily review is a great tool to get in touch with ourselves.

During your review, look at the five precepts and see if you are adhering to them. Remember, they are suggestions on how to act, not a list of commandments, so don't beat yourself up if you are not following them to the letter. We all have to decide just how far we go with them.

As the precepts are there to help us have a clear conscience and live a blameless life, it is good for us to know exactly where we are in implementing them. This will show us where to concentrate our efforts. I suggest you review the precepts regularly.

6
Social Principles

AT THIS POINT we have built the foundation and the pillars of our house, so now it's time to build the walls. These social principles take us further into our journey of becoming more responsible and reducing our suffering. By implementing these principles we will also be reducing the suffering of those around us. This is not a selfish journey; it is one that helps us gain compassion for others. But gaining compassion isn't enough. We have to reflect on the principles and put what we learn into practice. The walls we are building are ones of kindness, empathy and responsibility.

14—Be charitable
What we are talking about here is generosity. This played a big part in Gautama Buddha's teachings, and he mentioned it on numerous occasions. In the Itivuttaka, a collection of 112 short discourses, he told us about the fruits of giving:

> 'If beings knew, as I know, the fruit of sharing gifts, they would not enjoy their use without

sharing them, nor would the taint of stinginess obsess the heart and stay there. Even if it were their last bite, their last morsel of food, they would not enjoy its use without sharing it, if there were anyone to receive it'.

So what are the fruits of being generous? For the giver, they help foster a clear conscience; help you build a good future; and make you compassionate and a respected person within society. It also gives you a great feeling of warmth, pleasure and satisfaction. Many people think we shouldn't receive anything in return for giving, but I believe this is not being totally honest. If we give a gift to a child and the child smiles warmly at you, you are going to feel happy inside. If you take a sick person to a hospital, he or she is going to be grateful and you will feel that you have done a good deed. So it is true that we receive something from giving, and there is no shame in that.

However, we shouldn't give just to receive these things. They should be looked upon as a by-product and not the purpose for giving. The Anguttara Nikaya states five types of rewards for giving:

> 'These are the five rewards of generosity: One is dear and appealing to people in society, one is admired by good people, one's good name is spread about, one does not stray from the rightful duties of the householder, and at the time of death, one reappears in a good destination'.

One of the key things generosity does is prevent us from becoming miserly. It gives us temporary relief from the pain of selfishness and stops us from becoming totally wrapped up in ourselves. When we are miserly we worry day and night about our wealth and belongings. We go to great lengths to protect them. We can't sleep at night worrying if someone will break in and steal them. We grow to mistrust others, and our mind is disturbed from the pressure of protecting our wealth. The miser is so scared of losing his wealth that he hordes it. In the Samyutta Nikaya, Gautama Buddha said:

> 'What the miser fears, that keeps him from giving, is the very danger that comes when he doesn't give'.

How true is that?

So a miser lives in fear of his wealth, but to what end? When we die we are not able to take anything with us, so isn't it nicer to give things away whilst we are alive? I am not talking about giving everything away and living as a pauper. But there is only so much wealth and belongings we need or can use.

If we do give, we have to be careful that our generosity stems from compassion and not from pride. Our intention and motivation are extremely important here. If you are giving just to get thanks or praise, it isn't going to benefit you in the ways I mentioned above. Your conscience is not going to be clear; you will not become more compassionate or reduce your suffering; and you certainly will not get respect from others. Giving something and expecting praise is not a very attractive trait.

How does generosity help clear our conscience and reduce our suffering? Well, Gautama Buddha's teachings are mainly concerned with our state of mind and generosity is about not being attached to or craving material things. He stated in the four truths that our suffering stems from our craving and attachment to things; without this craving and attachment our minds become clearer, happier and a little freer, which in turn means less suffering. The Dana Sutra states three mental factors of giving:

> 'The donor, before giving, is glad; while giving, his/her mind is inspired; and after giving, is gratified'.

Gautama Buddha mentioned three different types of giving. The first covers giving something away we no longer want. This doesn't ask much of us as we have already finished with the thing we are giving away, such as old clothes and books. This is a kind of recycling.

The second is giving away something that we would like to receive ourselves, such as new clothes, the latest mobile phone, book or CD. There is a lot of thoughtfulness and caring in this type of giving.

The third type is giving away something that is very dear to us, such as a painting we cherish or some personal jewellery. This type of giving shows that we are not attached to something and understand its impermanence. This is the most difficult for us to engage in.

Giving doesn't just mean material things. It could be a friendly smile or kind, encouraging words. But whatever you are giving, you have to be sure it doesn't conflict with the precepts or any other code of ethics.

Whatever type of giving you are doing, do it with an open heart. Do not expect praise and thanks. Let the smile on the person's face be all the thanks you need.

Reflection

1. Think of a time when someone was generous towards you. How did it feel? Sit with that feeling for a moment. The warmth you are feeling now is the warmth others will feel when you are generous towards them.
2. Think of a time when you were generous towards someone. How did that feel? Hold on to that feeling and let it be your driving force for future generosity.

15—Practice virtuous actions
In principle 9 I mentioned the five precepts. These were discussed as things to refrain from, but instead of just avoiding negative actions, we should attempt to act in a positive and virtuous way. A good way to do this is to follow the positive aspects of the five precepts:

Practice harmlessness
Practice generosity

Practice faithfulness
Practice truthfulness
Practice self-control

Harmlessness—If our minds are filled with empathy and respect for all beings, we will never have the intention to harm anyone. We will see that others have difficulties and problems just like us. They go through life trying to be as happy as they can.

In our lives we see people who are less fortunate than ourselves, but instead of just having pity for them, we should have empathy. This is when we put ourselves in their shoes, see the world through their eyes and not try to fit their experience into our world view.

Empathy can be a real eye opener, and from it we can build compassion—not a compassion built on sorrow or guilt, but real heartfelt compassion. Once we have this type of compassion, it will become more difficult for us to have harmful thoughts.

When I lived in London I worked as a counsellor for a children's charity. We dealt with children up to the age of sixteen years who had been bullied, abused, or were going through a bad time at home or school. This is where I realised the true benefit of empathy. Once the child understands that you are not only listening to them, but you also are actually seeing their problems through their eyes, they start to relax and open up to you. It is then we can truly help them through their troubled times.

We are all different, and so people will always do and say things we may not agree with. But instead of becoming angry, we should respect their viewpoint and mentally thank them for showing us an alternative way of being. We may in the end not change our viewpoint, but at least we have shown the other person respect, and this means we will not have caused them any harm.

Generosity—This was covered in the previous principle.

Faithfulness—If we have a partner, we should be faithful to him or her. It is our responsibility to be kind and caring towards our partner, and vice versa. If we love and cherish someone, we will not want to cause that person any pain and suffering. If we have strong negative feelings towards a partner, I would suggest it is time to move on or at least talk it through. I am not saying we should give up at the first hurdle, but if something is over, it is over, and the kindest thing to do is to be honest. I think a huge part of faithfulness is honesty. Things may not always be sweetness and light between you, but if you are honest, things may work themselves out.

It seems to be a strong human trait to want what we don't have. We seem never to be satisfied. The grass is always greener on the other side, until you reach the other side, and then you find some other patch of grass to desire. If we were talking about smartphones here, no harm is done, but we are talking about other humans, who have feelings. If we think how cruel unfaithfulness is, we would never consider being unfaithful.

Faithfulness is concerned not only with partners; it also covers work colleagues, parents, family, friends and anyone else you come into contact with. Being faithful means to be trustworthy, loyal and steadfast. Is that you?

Truthfulness—The saying goes, "honesty is the best policy," and it clearly is. We hate to be lied to and so does everyone else. When we are truthful we gain respect, friends and trust. I believe we all long for these things.

We also gain a mind that is calm, without guilt and remorse. Sometimes the truth is painful, but being lied to is more painful.

Self-control—Once we drink too much, take illegal drugs, are overcome by sexual urges or are angry, our self-control goes out the window, and with it the previous four precepts.

Self-control is nothing more than mindfulness. If we are mindful of our thoughts, our speech and our bodily actions, we will stay in control. However, once we have lost control of our mind, our speech and actions follow suit. Self-control helps us be sure that our behaviour and impulses are kept in check.

This is an alternative way of looking at the precepts. If we keep harmlessness, generosity, faithfulness, truthfulness and self-control in the forefront of our minds, we will be practicing virtuous actions. Let these five be the benchmarks in our daily review sessions.

Reflection

1. Are you a virtuous person? Do you follow the five positive precepts? As always, be honest. Look at the areas where you are the weakest and consider how you can improve. You can start this process here, but carry it on in your daily life by staying mindful.

16—Help your friends and relatives
In principles 11 and 12 we spoke about helping our parents/guardians and spouse/children. However, we shouldn't stop there; we should also help our friends and extended family. As we help one another we create goodwill, and this will help us along the path.

As with our parents, we can help people materially, financially, physically or emotionally. Sometimes emotional help is the most important. There are times in all our lives when we feel like we have hit rock bottom. It is at these times we need a shoulder to cry on or a helping hand.

Remember what I said previously about cause and effect? If we help people when they need assistance, they are more likely to help us when we are in trouble. So it is of great benefit to all of us to help each other. We all grow stronger with mutual help and support.

It is important to help our friends, but it is equally important to choose good friends. Here is a quote attributed to Gautama Buddha that sums up the importance of choosing one's friends carefully:

> 'An insincere and evil friend is more to be feared than a wild beast; a wild beast may wound your body, but an evil friend will wound your mind'.

So be sure you surround yourself with good friends, and once you have done that, strive to be a good friend yourself. Let me finish by mentioning what it says about a true friend in the Mitta Sutra:

> 'He gives what is beautiful, hard to give, does what is hard to do, endures painful, ill-spoken words. His secrets he tells you, your secrets he keeps. When misfortunes strike, he doesn't abandon you; when you're down and out, doesn't look down on you. A person in whom these traits are found, is a friend to be cultivated by anyone wanting a friend'.

We should not only try to look for friends like this, but also try to become that type of friend ourselves.

Reflection

1. Think of a time when you needed help and someone was there for you. Sit with those feelings. I am sure you were grateful for this help, and this is how others will feel when you help them.
2. There may have been a time in your life when you needed help and no help came. Sit with those

feelings. If it has never happened to you, just imagine what it would be like. You are probably feeling sad and letdown. Let these feelings spur you on to help your friends and relatives—in fact, everyone you come into contact with.

17—Be blameless in your conduct
A blameless life is one whereby we do not harm other beings with our body, speech or mind. In fact, we go out of our way to help others, and that includes animals and the environment.

What these principles are trying to do is reduce our sense of unease and discontentment with life, and the way they are doing it is to show us that by being kind, caring and blameless we will have less stress and guilt, and our minds will be more stable and less agitated. I am sure we would all welcome that.

As you work through these principles, you will see that some are about helping yourself directly—such as following an ethical code and learning practical skills—and some are about helping others—such as taking care of your spouse and helping your friends. This is because we do not live in a bubble. We are all interconnected. So if you help others and live a blameless life, you are indirectly helping yourself. But if you harm others and live a blameworthy life, you are in turn harming yourself. This is what I was saying at the beginning of the book: we are all in this together.

A great way to help others is to do volunteer work. I am sure we can find some time in our busy lives to help others. It doesn't have to be working for a recognised charity. It could be helping needy people in your community: mowing the lawn for an old person, taking a sick neighbour to hospital, raising funds for local charities and so on. You will be surprised at the difference you can make if you try.

If you are so busy you have no time for others, then try to give money, clothes, books, etc., to charities. We have to try our best to take our practice off the cushion and out into the community. It is of course a great benefit to meditate on compassion, but if that is all we are doing, we will not be able to bring about a sea of change in the way we think and act.

In the Kalama Sutra, Gautama Buddha mentioned another aspect of a blameless life:

> 'And this undeluded person, not overcome by delusion, his mind not possessed by delusion, doesn't kill living beings, take what is not given, go after another person's wife, tell lies or induce others to do likewise, all of which is for long-term welfare and happiness.
>
> 'So what do you think, Kalamas: Are these qualities blameworthy or blameless?'
>
> 'Blameless'.

What he is saying here is that if we follow the five precepts, we will already be on the road to living a blameless life. It may not be enough, but it certainly is a great starting point.

We must stay aware, moment by moment, of our actions of body, speech and mind. If we do not have thoughts of ill will, do not tell lies or use words that will harm others and do not kill, steal or otherwise hurt people and animals, then we truly are blameless.

It is also important not to encourage others to act against the five precepts. If we can teach and encourage others to follow a blameless path, we will be doing a great service to humankind, and our lives will become blameless and beyond reproach. I actually see it as my duty as a teacher, so I always encourage moral behaviour in my teachings.

Reflection

1. Revisit the five precepts and see how much progress you have made since principle 9. Redouble your efforts to follow these five and lead a blameless life.
2. Do you help others? If so, think about the difference you are making. This is not to build pride, but to show you what a blameless life looks like. If you do not help others, think about the ways you could help—then make a commitment to start helping.

In one of your daily reviews, think about your life. Are you blameless? Can we be totally blameless in today's society? Are there areas to work on? If there are, set yourself some goals and start working towards them. Check back regularly to follow your progress.

18—Refrain from harmful acts

If we do not want to disturb our minds, we have to be sure we go through life not harming others. Once we start harming others, we release a Pandora's box of emotions and feelings within ourselves. So harmful acts are not good for us or others—nobody wins.

So how do we know what constitutes harmful acts? Gautama Buddha, in the Saleyyaka Sutra, mentioned ten harmful acts to steer clear of. They are divided into three aspects: three for bodily acts, four for speech and three for mind. These ten harmful acts cover what we think, say and do. The opposite of the ten harmful acts are the ten helpful acts. I will mention the helpful acts at the end of each harmful act. Let's look at the three parts individually:

> 'And how are there three kinds of bodily conduct not in accordance with harmless conduct? Here someone is a killer of living beings: he is murderous, bloody-handed, given to blows and violence, and merciless to all living beings. He is a taker of what is not given: he takes as a thief takes another's chattels and property in the village or in the forest. He is given over to misconduct in sexual desires: he has intercourse with such women as are protected by their mother, father, brother, sister, relatives or husband, and also with those

who are betrothed. That is how there are three kinds of bodily conduct not in accordance with harmless conduct'.

So the ways we harm others with our bodily actions are through killing, stealing and sexual misconduct. All of these have been covered in principle 9. The helpful aspect of these three are: instead of killing, have compassion; instead of stealing, be generous; instead of sexual misconduct, have self-control and follow a code of ethics.

'And how are there four kinds of verbal conduct not in accordance with harmless conduct? Here someone speaks falsehood: when summoned to a court or to a meeting, or to his relatives' presence, or to his guild, or to the royal family's presence, and questioned as a witness thus, "So, good man, tell what you know," then, not knowing, he says "I know," or knowing, he says "I do not know," not seeing, he says "I see," or seeing, he says "I do not see"; in full awareness he speaks falsehood for his own ends or for another's ends or for some trifling worldly end. He speaks divisively: he is a repeater elsewhere of what is heard here for the purpose of causing division from these, or he is a repeater to these of what is heard elsewhere for the purpose of causing division from those, and he is thus a divider of the united, a creator of divisions, who enjoys discord, rejoices in discord, delights in discord, he is a speaker of words that create discord. He speaks harshly: he utters such words as are rough, hard, hurtful to others, censorious of others, bordering on anger and not conducive to concentration. He is a gossip: as one who tells that which is unseasonable, that which is not fact, that which is not good, that which is not the Gautama Buddha's teachings, that which is not the discipline, and he speaks out of season speech not worth recording, which is unreasoned, indefinite, and unconnected with good. That is how there are four kinds of verbal conduct not in accordance with harmless conduct'.

Lying has been covered in principle 9, and divisive speech, harsh words and gossiping have been covered in principle 10. Look back to remind yourself.

The positive side to these four are: instead of lying, speak only the truth; instead of being divisive, speak kind words that bring people together; instead of using harsh words, use pleasing words; and instead of wasting your time gossiping, speak only meaningful and encouraging words.

'And how are there three kinds of mental conduct not in accordance with harmless conduct? Here someone is covetous: he is a coveter of another's chattels and property thus: "Oh, that what is another's were mine!" Or he has a mind of ill will, with the intention of a mind affected by hate thus: "May these beings be slain and slaughtered, may they be cut off, perish, or be annihilated!" Or he has inappropriate view, distorted vision, thus: "There is nothing given, nothing offered, nothing sacrificed, no fruit and ripening of good and bad actions." That is how there are three kinds of mental conduct not in accordance with harmless conduct'.

Covetousness—this is born out of greed and desire; it is when we want what someone else has. Instead of being happy that someone has something new, we selfishly want it for ourselves. It may not be a material thing we desire; it may be wealth or another person. This way of thinking brings us only dissatisfaction. We may be able to outwardly pretend we are happy for what others have, but inwardly we are burning with covetousness and ill will.

I can remember when I was young and the boy next door had a new bike. It was brand new and everyone commented on it. I coveted it day and night. I couldn't stop thinking about it because I didn't have a bike of my own and I really wanted one. The thought of his bike consumed me so much I couldn't think straight. One day I let the air out of his tyres because I thought if I can't ride it, neither can he. This is how you become when you covet things. It can lead to ill will, jealousy, lying and so on.

Ill will—this has been written about in Chapter One. Again, I would encourage you to go back to familiarise yourself with the concept, because it is from these bad thoughts that bad actions materialise.

Inappropriate view—the inappropriate view we are talking about here is a view whereby you believe that acts do not have consequences. You think it doesn't matter what you do because nothing is going to come of it. You have no regard for cause and effect or interconnectedness.

You also believe that things are permanent and true happiness can be found in material things, even though everything around you points to the opposite of this.

You feel there is a solid permanent self—this point will be addressed in principle 36.

You don't believe you are suffering and so are not interested in following a path that may lead to a reduction in that suffering.

The helpful side to these three are: instead of coveting what others have, be satisfied and contented; instead of having ill will, have goodwill by thinking kind and helpful thoughts, as these will lead to good and helpful actions; instead of having an inappropriate view, study Gautama Buddha's teachings, clear up any doubts, meditate on what you have learnt and then implement them as this will lead to you having an appropriate view.

That brings us to the end of the ten harmful acts that we have to try and refrain from doing as they disturb our minds and cause us to act in a way that will harm others.

I think it is important to mention here that we should not only endeavour to follow the ten helpful acts ourselves, but should also help others by promoting the virtue of following them. Gautama Buddha said in the Chavalata Sutra that a person that doesn't promote good acts for themselves and others is like a piece of wood from a pyre: burnt at both ends and in the middle fouled with dung, because it serves neither for fuel in the village, nor timber in the forest. In other words, it is not of much use. So if we know about these ten helpful acts but decide not to implement them and promote them to others, we are just like that piece of wood: we are not helping ourselves or others.

Reflection

1. Think about these ten harmful acts individually, and see which ones you need to work on. It may be that you have to work on all of them to differing degrees. So be sure you become fully aware of them, as you can use them later in your daily review. Think about what harm they cause you and those around you. Again, give this much thought as it will become one of your drivers for change.

In your daily review look back over your day and see how many of these ten you refrained from and how many you didn't. Write down the ones that seem more difficult to avoid. Then look at why that is; what or who do you believe is stopping you? What feelings and emotions arise when you think about them? Once you understand the root cause, you will be able to let the feelings and emotions be. It may take a while, so work on only one at a time. Once you have brought the awareness of why you are not able to avoid the action, you must take that awareness into your daily life. I will talk about how to do that in the next principle.

19—Great effort

In the last principle we looked at what ten harmful acts we had to refrain from and what their counterparts were. Now we will look at the effort we have to put into avoiding the harmful acts and developing the helpful ones. Here is a list to make it easier for you to remember what these acts are.

Harmful	**Helpful**
1. Killing	Compassion
2. Stealing	Generosity
3. Sexual misconduct	Self-control
4. Lying	Truthfulness
5. Divisive speech	Kind speech
6. Harsh words	Pleasant words
7. Gossiping	Helpful words
8. Covetousness	Contentment
9. Ill will	Goodwill
10. Inappropriate view	Appropriate view

Gautama Buddha spoke about four great efforts: the effort to avoid, the effort to overcome, the effort to develop and the effort to maintain.

The effort to avoid
The first effort is to prevent harmful actions and emotions that have not yet arisen.

These harmful potential actions disturb our minds and the minds of others around us. So we have to make the effort to avoid arousing them.

A big obstacle that hinders our effort and concentration, and so make it difficult to stop the arousal of harmful states, are the five hindrances. These were spoken about in Chapter One, but by way of a reminder here are the five, which Gautama Buddha taught in the Vitakkasanthana Sutra:

> We are stupefied by sensual desire—craving for and attachment to such things as sense pleasures, wealth, respect, power and fame.

> We burn with ill will—anger, hatred, resentment, jealousy and repulsion. These thoughts can be aimed at people, objects, situations and even oneself.

> We fall into apathy and laziness—the first makes it difficult to arouse our interest in anything. The second produces heaviness of mind and a sleepiness. Both of these make it difficult to direct our effort towards something.

We are anxious—this makes you tense and irritable. You are unable to concentrate on anything other than your problems.

We have doubt—lacking full confidence in what we are doing and wondering if it will even work. We have difficulty marrying our experiences with what is being said.

What is the connection between harmful actions, emotions that have not yet arisen and hindrances? Usually, hindrances are activated when your senses come into contact with sense objects, such as eye to form, ear to sound and so on. The mind deals with these impressions in different ways—sometimes positive, sometimes negative and sometimes neutral. When it deals with them in a positive or neutral way, there is no problem regarding harmful thoughts, feelings and emotions (although positive impressions may lead to overexcitement). However, when it deals with them in a negative way, these sense objects stir up harmful thoughts, feelings and emotions.

We have to become aware of the hindrances that are stopping us from arousing helpful states. Once we have done that, we can implement the antidotes to these hindrances. The antidotes can be found in Chapter One. These will stop the five hindrances in their track and, in turn, prevent any harmful thoughts and emotions from arising.

Do a daily review and see what hindrances you had. Then think what it would have been like if you had applied the antidotes. Next time the hindrance arises, try to apply the antidote. You can do this by staying aware of your emotions and actions.

The effort to overcome
The first effort stopped harmful actions and emotions from arising, whereas this effort is to overcome the harmful states that have already arisen. In the Anguttara Nikaya, Gautama Buddha says that we should abandon the harmful states, dispel them, destroy them and cause them to disappear. But how? In the Majjhima Nikaya, he gave five techniques to help us do this. They are:

1. Chase away the harmful thought with a helpful one. This can be done during the daily review session. If you have been in the grip of harmful thoughts and emotions during the day, try using one of the these reflections:

    a) Sensual desires can be overcome by reflecting on the impermanence of things.
    b) Ill will can be overcome by reflecting that all beings want happiness and to reduce their suffering.
    c) Lack of interest or laziness can be overcome by stopping what you are doing, be it studying or reflecting, and going for a walk, splashing water on your face, doing simple stretching exercises or, my favourite, simply having a cup of tea.

d) Anxiousness can be overcome through the breathing meditation in Chapter One. This will help you become more relaxed and focused.
e) Doubt can be overcome by simply asking questions and investigating.

Thus it is extremely important to chase away unhelpful thoughts and emotions.

2. Regret—we are not talking about guilt here; that is quite a different thing. Regret does not mean beating yourself up over something you have done.

    Here we must reflect on our harmful actions and build up a kind of revulsion that will stop us from doing these actions again. It is not enough to just commit ourselves to stopping these actions; we have to make an effort not to do them again. It is a bit stupid to feel remorse for our harmful actions and then do exactly the same thing again. Our effort must be focused on never repeating these harmful actions.

3. Divert your attention. When a harmful thought arises, do not indulge in it. If you are walking down the street and you see the latest smartphone, a person you are angry with, the car of your dreams or some other sense object you are craving, you should simply turn away. Look in the other direction or think about something else, as this will

avert any unhelpful thoughts and emotions that may arise. Of course, this is easier said than done.

4. Confrontation. This technique is the opposite of the third one: Confront the harmful thought head-on. Do not shy away from it. Look at it and see where it came from. By doing this, the thought will eventually disappear. This confrontation may be difficult to do at the time, so it can be done at your daily review session. Once you get more experienced, you can confront the harmful thought as it arises.

5. Suppression. A note of caution: In my experience, when you suppress things you are just storing up trouble for the future. If you suppress a bad experience or a powerful emotion, it will resurface, much stronger, later on. This technique is my least favourite and must be used only as a last resort, but I hope the other four techniques would have already worked for you.

These are the five techniques to overcome our harmful thoughts and emotions that have already arisen, as taught by Gautama Buddha. First experience these antidotes at your daily review sessions. Get comfortable with them and try to use them as soon as the harmful thought or emotion arises.

The effort to develop
The third effort is to develop helpful qualities that have not as yet arisen. This is where you should make an effort

to develop thoughts and actions such as generosity, patience, an ethical code, empathy and compassion.

Again, the perfect time to think about and cultivate these helpful states is during your daily review session. If you review each day which thoughts and actions have been helpful and which have been harmful, you will see a pattern emerge. You will be able to see what you need to work on and make into a kind of habit.

Remember that we are trying to live a responsible life that disturbs neither our mind nor the minds of others.

What is really needed is honesty. We must be completely truthful with ourselves and investigate which helpful states we do not have, and then put all our effort into cultivating them.

During a daily review session, write down the ten helpful acts on a piece of paper. Then grade them from one to ten—ten being the state that comes naturally to you and one being the state with which you have to work really hard to cultivate. Those you grade from one to five are the ones you should work on. At regular intervals, do the grading again. Note your progress every time and recommit to developing the helpful states you do not yet have.

This is how we can develop helpful states that have not yet arisen.

The effort to maintain
The fourth and final effort is to maintain the helpful states that have already arisen.

This follows on from the previous effort. There, you contemplated which helpful states you didn't have. Now you must focus on the ones you do have. You should remain mindful at all times of these helpful states so they can become a habit. It is no good lying sometimes and telling the truth at others; stealing sometimes and not stealing other times; getting totally drunk one day and then saying you don't drink another day; or being faithful sometimes and cheating on your partner at other times. These helpful states must become natural and spontaneous. You have to put a great amount of effort into keeping these helpful states going, because if you do not stay aware, they can easily drift away from you. Awareness is the key here.

Be happy that you have these helpful states and give yourself a pat on the back—I mean it, because it shows that you are on the right path to living responsibly, which in turn should help increase your self-esteem and confidence.

Look at the list you made in the last section and note the helpful states you graded between six and ten. Check to see if you really have achieved them, and they are not just what you wish you had achieved. Be truthful! If you truly have them, then stay mindful, and direct your effort towards maintaining them.

Let us summarise the main points here: We have to avoid harmful states that have not yet arisen; overcome the harmful states that have arisen; develop helpful states that have not yet arisen; and maintain the helpful states that have arisen. This is where we should be concentrating our effort in our daily review sessions.

Reflection

1. Look very carefully at the ten harmful and helpful acts and the four great efforts. Think long and hard about them. What I want you to do is remember them. This may seem like being back at school, but I want you to keep them at the forefront of your mind during the day; memorising them will help. This will show you when you need to avoid, overcome, develop or maintain a certain state.

20—Refrain from intoxicants
This has been covered in principle 9, but I would just add here that drinking alcohol and taking illegal drugs are the cause of some deep-rooted problems in society. In many countries, alcohol and illegal drugs are major factors in domestic violence, crime and road death tolls. They also contribute to hospital A&E departments being full on weekends. They damage your liver and heart and contribute to diabetes. They destroy families, friendships, marriages and lives. They are a major problem, and this is why this precept makes so much sense.

People seem to think they need alcohol or illegal drugs to have fun and be social. This clearly is not the case; instead of helping you, they could end up destroying you and the people around you. When we are under the influence of alcohol and illegal drugs, we lose control of our body, speech and mind. How then can we be sure we are refraining from the other four precepts or the ten harmful acts if we can't even think straight?

Reflection

1. 1. Think of the dangers of alcohol and illegal drugs. Have they destroyed people you know? Have they caused you distress in the past? Can you think and act straight when you are under the influence? By thinking about these points you will fully understand this precept.

21—Be diligent in your practice
Gautama Buddha's last words were along the lines of 'attain the goal by diligence'. Some may use words like *heedfully, untiringly, earnestly* or *mindfully*. I prefer the word *diligent*, but please feel free to substitute the word you like best.

Now he could have said some inspiring words about enlightenment, rebirth or karma, but he chose to give us some advice instead, and that advice stated that we should be diligent in our practice because that is the way we will be able to reduce our suffering.

This wasn't the only time he mentioned being diligent. In the Appamada Sutra, he said:

> 'Just as the rafters in a peak-roofed house all go to the roof-peak, incline to the roof-peak, converge at the roof-peak and the roof-peak is reckoned the foremost among them; in the same way, all skilful qualities are rooted in diligence, converge in diligence and diligence is reckoned the foremost among them'.

So it is clear that we have to be diligent about our practice. In the Upajjhatthana Sutra he mentioned five things we should reflect on regularly, and I believe if we do, we will be able to stay diligent in whatever practice we follow—in fact, in everything we do from moment to moment. This is because we will be seeing things as they are and not through rose-coloured spectacles. The five things we should reflect on regularly are:

1. I am subject to ageing.
2. I am subject to illness.
3. I am subject to death.
4. I will grow separate from all that is dear and appealing to me.
5. I am the owner of my actions, heir to my actions.

The first three—ageing, sickness and death—are very apparent in our daily lives, and so should be easy to reflect on.

Why does number 4 say, 'I will grow separate from all that is dear and appealing to me'? It is because nothing is permanent and everything changes, so family, friends and loved ones will not be with us forever. Also, the material things we cherish so much are impermanent and so will not last. If we reflect on this point it will stop us from becoming attached to people and things.

Number 5 is talking about cause and effect. Remember that our actions are like an echo and will return to us at a later stage. Reflection on this point will help ensure that our actions are kind, helpful and blameless.

Reflection on all of these will help you remain diligent. I would suggest you periodically work them into your daily review session.

• • •

As we have now reached the end of this section and are over half way through, I would like you to review what we have covered so you can stay diligent with the practices I have introduced. After that, you will be ready to move on to the next half of this book.

Below I have posed some questions that I would like you to reflect on:.

- How do people who exert a negative influence on you affect your thoughts and emotions? How do

ones that exert a positive influence affect your thoughts and emotions?
- Do you believe it is important to show respect to those that have earned it? If so, why? What are the benefits to them and you?
- Does your location affect the way you think, feel and act? If so, in what way?
- Do your past actions colour your world today? Are there consequences to your actions?
- Gautama Buddha spoke about an 'appropriate path'. What are you looking for in your chosen path? Have you found an appropriate path? Is it fulfilling your needs?
- How many of the five precepts do you regularly adhere to? Are you making improvements in this area?
- Does people's speech affect you? Do your words affect them?
- Why is it important to help your parents, spouse, children, relatives and friends?
- How do you think being charitable is going to help others? Could you be more generous?
- Which of the ten harmful acts that have not yet arisen do you have to avoid, and which ones that have arisen do you have to overcome?
- Which of the ten helpful acts do you have to develop because they have not yet arisen, and which ones do you have to maintain?
- Were these questions easy to reflect on? If not, why? Was it because of one or more of the five

hindrances? Think about it. Think about each of the hindrances and see how they affect your life.

I hope these questions have helped you focus on what we have covered so far. Please remain focused and diligent throughout the rest of this book, because that is the way you will be able to get the most out of it.

Summary
Once we have worked through these social principles, we should have a clear understanding of who Gautama Buddha advised us to be. He envisaged each of us as a charitable and generous person; someone who is virtuous, blameless and diligent in his or her practice and life; someone who not only knows the difference between harmful and helpful acts, but also puts great effort into ensuring that his or her acts do not harm anyone; a person who has self-control where intoxicants are concerned.

By completing this set of principles, you would have gone a long way towards achieving your goal of becoming a more responsible person, which, in turn, will help reduce a large part of your suffering.

7
Individual Principles

TO CARRY ON the metaphor of building a house, we have now come to the part where we fit the windows and doors. The preliminary work has been finished, and now we are starting to fill in the gaps.

This next set of principles will build on what we have already achieved; it will lead us closer to our goal of reducing suffering and increasing our responsibility within society. It will show us how we, as responsible, caring people, should act.

22—Venerate those worthy of it
I am going to start this principle with a reflection. Whom do you venerate? Why are they worthy of it?

I ask these questions because everyone's answers are going to be different. We all venerate people for different reasons. It is no point me giving you a long list of people to venerate and tell you why I think they are worthy.

The benefit of venerating someone who is worthy of it is to reduce your pride and stop you from being conceited. It is also to show respect to someone who has helped you or shown you the way. I know some people find it very hard to venerate others. If that is the case with you, I would suggest you spend some time during your daily review session thinking about why that is.

Others are too free with their veneration. Tell them this person has a title or is some higher being, and they will instantly bow down and shower that person with money and gifts. The danger here is we are leaving ourselves vulnerable and open to abuse. No matter what people say, these people are only human and so are fallible like us and liable to make mistakes.

When I was studying Buddhist philosophy in Nepal, I had an excellent teacher. He had over twelve years of intensive retreat and he taught from his experiences and personal understanding of Buddhism, and not from books. I was in awe of him and thought I was in the company of someone really special, a higher being perhaps. These were my projections and not something he encouraged or even wanted.

One day whilst teaching, he said that women cannot become a Buddha. If you want to be a Buddha, you have to be born a man. I was devastated. How could such an enlightened being say, what seemed to me, such chauvinistic things? What made it worst was he was not willing to debate it or even offer any proof.

I felt let down and cheated, but that wasn't his fault—it was mine. I had built him up to be someone he wasn't. So please be careful that your veneration isn't you just projecting something on to someone that isn't actually there.

A person worthy of veneration is someone whose words match his or her actions. There are many people out there who speak sweet words, but when you look at their actions, they just don't match. *Dhammapada,* verse 51, states:

> 'Like a beautiful flower full of colour but without fragrance, even so, fruitless are the fair words of one who does not practice them'.

What is needed is a person of integrity. This is a person who is honest and has moral soundness. Gautama Buddha, in the Sappurisa Sutra, mentioned the quality of a person with no integrity:

> 'There is the case where a person of no integrity goes forth from a high-ranking family. He notices, "I have gone forth from a high-ranking family, but these other people have not gone forth from a high-ranking family." He praises himself for having a high-ranking family and belittles others. This is the quality of a person of no integrity'.

People of integrity neither praise themselves nor belittle others. This really is someone to venerate.

Reflection

1. Think about these questions again. Whom do you venerate? Why are they worthy of it? See if you still feel the same or have you realised you are just projecting qualities onto someone that doesn't have them.

23—Be humble
I always feel that a humble person is easy to be around. They do not waste time bragging about what they have, who they are, or where they have been. They play down their achievements and are more attentive to others' needs.

The opposite of this is someone who is proud and conceited. These are not attractive traits. It is difficult for me to spend much time with someone who boasts. They are only interested in selling themselves and have no interest in who you are or what you think or know.

I have always found people with pride to also have the biggest egos—and usually the biggest mouths to go with them. But a humble person is quiet, respectful and attentive. Which one would you rather be around? Which one would you rather be?

Another trait of proud and conceited people is that they are not open-minded nor willing to learn from others, as they think they already know everything. Now this is something we have to guard against while moving along this meandering path. If we start to think we are making great progress and are already better than the people around us, we are going to run up against obstacles such as pride.

We have to stay open-minded. Just because we know a way to do something, it doesn't mean another person doesn't know a better or easier way. We shouldn't assume we know best. Humble people will continue to learn throughout their lives.

Once we become proud and egotistical, it is very hard to subdue these emotions. So it is better not to travel down that road in the first place.

We have to also be mindful of people praising us. They may be flattering you because of your position or they want something. However, it may be that you are worthy of praise, but be careful: our ego loves to be praised, and it may lead to pride if we are not mindful.

So what are the causes of pride? There are many, but two main causes are dualistic thinking and an inflated sense of self.

When people think in a dualistic way, it can stir up pride because they start thinking I am good and others are bad; I'm handsome, they are ugly; I'm intelligent and they are stupid. It is this type of thinking that causes us to fixate on 'I am this', 'I am that'. We start to emphasise the sense of self, which leads us to become attached to who we think we are. Both of these lead to pride and conceit. In the Nipata Sutra, Gautama Buddha stated this:

> 'By being alert and attentive, he begins to let go of cravings as they arise. But whatever he begins to accomplish, he should beware of inner pride. He must avoid thinking of himself as better than another, or worse or equal, for that is all comparison and emphasises the self'.

'The Thirty-seven Practices of a Bodhisattva' advises us how we should act, even if we are rich or famous:

> Even when you are famous, honoured by all and as rich as the god of wealth himself, know that success in the world is ephemeral and don't let it go to your head—this is the practice of a bodhisattva.

(Translation by Ken McLeod from his book *Reflections on Silver River*. A bodhisattva, as explained in this excellent book, is a person who lives and breathes compassion.)

So it is clear that humility is a trait we have to work at, or we could find ourselves getting wrapped up in pride. The pride I am talking about here is our overinflated sense of self. It is not the pride we have for our children, loved ones and so on, which stems from love and compassion; this overinflated sense of self pride stems from our ego.

Reflection

1. Think of people you know or have met who are full of pride. How do they make you feel? Now think of a humble person, and see how he or she makes you feel. What is the difference in your feelings?
2. Why do you think Gautama Buddha stated that we should be humble? What are the advantages? Are you humble? I expect we never look at these points, so give them a lot of thought.

In a daily review session look at pride and humility. Which one do you lean towards? Think back over the last few days and see what situations stir up pride in you, and which ones make you humble. Only when we become focused on these situations are we able to change.

Final words for you to reflect on:

> 'Why take pride in this body and in possessions, they do not last. They are like castles in the sand swept away by the tide; like the scent of a flower carried off by the wind'.

24—Be content

Oh, to be content. If only we could, but it seems human beings have a natural urge to never be content. Or can we? We have to look at what is need and what is greed. I think we can satisfy our need, but we will never satisfy our greed.

What we need is food, clothes, work, money and human contact. These bring us security and are things we are able to satisfy to some degree.

What we want is the latest smartphone, expensive clothes, big cars, huge houses, exotic holidays—in short, we want to not only fit in with society, we also want to stand out.

We have to train ourselves to know when enough is enough. If we just blindly follow our desire to want more, we will never be content. We have to think carefully to see if we really need something, or are we just trying to buy happiness. That is a fool's game. If we buy something to be happy, it will not last. As soon as a new version comes out or the thing breaks, we will become unhappy and discontented. To try and buy happiness is like drinking saltwater to quench your thirst—it will only lead to dissatisfaction. Just think that if you could buy happiness, all rich people would be totally content, but they are not. They are just like the rest of us, always searching for something to make them happier.

The desire to want more and more brings us anxiety, worry and stress, whereas contentment can bring us peace of mind and calmness. The fear of losing our happiness leads us to frantically search for more happiness. What we see is that people are unable to be content with themselves or what they have. They are constantly craving new things, but once they obtain them they suffer from loss, dissatisfaction and discontent. When they cannot obtain the thing of their desire they become sad and angry; disappointment and despair set in. There are two main reasons for this type of suffering. One is our inability to be content with the present moment. The other is when we make our happiness dependent on someone or something outside us. Our discontent leads us to have more desires in the hope of escaping these types of suffering.

I remember when I became a monk and stopped chasing material happiness: I felt a stillness and relaxation of the mind. I had been living in London and like everyone else was chasing the dream—whatever that was. I had a three-storey house, large SUV and more clothes than I could ever wear, but was I content? No. I feel more content and secure now that I only have as much as I need.

Everyone's needs are different and so we have to personally decide what is required. This can be done at a daily review session. If you are yearning for something, think if it fills a need or just your greed. But as I have mentioned throughout this book, be honest!

A note of caution: we shouldn't take contentment to mean we don't have to put in the effort to better ourselves—of course we do. We have to find our own level of contentment and once we do, it will be better than any wealth or material belongings.

Gautama Buddha says in the *Dhammapada*, verse 203:

'...contentment is the greatest wealth'.

Reflection

1. Are you content? Do you have enough to satisfy your needs? Do you chase after happiness in material things? Do new things bring you happiness? How long does it last? Give all of these points a lot of thought.

25—Be grateful

Gratitude means to be thankful for and remember the help others have given us. We should also try our best to pay back any help we have received if and when the person who has helped us needs it.

In the Dullabha Sutra it states:

> 'These two people are hard to find in the world. Which two? The one who is first to do a kindness, and the one who is grateful for a kindness done and feels obligated to repay it. These two people are hard to find in the world'.

These days people seem to have very short memories where being grateful is concerned. Gratitude is a virtue we should do our best to cultivate.

That is the first part of this principle. The second part involves the original Pali word *Katannuta*. It has been translated as *gratitude*, but this doesn't quite cover it. It literally means that you know what someone has done for your benefit. So instead of it being an emotional thing as gratitude is usually seen to be—for example, we say things like 'I feel grateful'—the literal meaning makes it more intellectual. This translation seems to involve an element of knowledge; we know what has been done for our benefit. So if we don't know what has been done for us, we will not be grateful.

This is an important point because it takes in the interconnectedness of everything. If we just sit down and eat our dinner without being aware of what we are eating, who planted and harvested it, who packaged and delivered it and so on, we will not be grateful. Being grateful is connected with an awareness of the world around us, how it works, and who is doing what to benefit us.

Reflect on this:

> 'A noble person is mindful and thankful for the favours he receives from others'.

So it isn't just a point of being grateful; we also have to been mindful of the interconnectedness of the world.

Reflection

1. Think of your last meal, and follow the process back from your plate to the seed in the ground. Think about all the people involved in the process. It could be a fairly long list. We should be grateful to all of these people because they have benefited us by providing food that we can eat.

26—Receive teachings at a favourable time

I believe the most favourable time is when we are able to fully connect with the teaching. I don't know about you, but I have sat through teachings and not really taken very much of them on board. I am physically there, but mentally I am off in my own world. So this undoubtedly isn't a favourable time.

Some people go to as many teachings as possible, thinking this is what being a Buddhist is all about. They believe that even if they don't listen or try to understand the teaching, it will leave an imprint on their mind for their next life. I know when I first moved to India, I spent a great part of my first few years at one teaching or another. I wasn't fully taking them in, and I certainly didn't give myself time to implement them. Buddhism was just an identity for me. So again, this was not a favourable time for me to receive any teachings.

We are humans, and we all like to belong to some group or club, whether it is a football team, religion, yoga club or gym—we all identify with something. However, Buddhism isn't really about identity; it is about changing oneself by implementing the teachings. Gautama Buddha gave some advice on this subject in an amusing discourse called Gadrabha Sutra:

> 'It is just as if a donkey were following right after a herd of cattle, saying, "I too am a cow! I too am a cow!" Its colour is not that of a cow, its voice is not that of a cow, its hoof is not that of a cow, and

yet it still keeps following right after the herd of cattle, saying, "I too am a cow! I too am a cow!"

'In the same way, there is the case where a certain person follows right after a community of Buddhists, saying, "I too am a Buddhist! I too am a Buddhist!" He doesn't have the other Buddhists' desire for undertaking the training in heightened virtue, doesn't have their desire for undertaking the training in heightened mind [concentration], doesn't have their desire for undertaking the training in heightened discernment, and yet he still keeps following right after the community of Buddhists, saying, "I too am a Buddhist! I too am a Buddhist!"

'So you should train yourselves: "Strong will be our desire for undertaking the training in heightened virtue; strong will be our desire for undertaking the training in heightened mind [concentration]; strong will be our desire for undertaking the training in heightened discernment." That is how you should train yourselves'.

So it isn't about an identity, accumulating teachings or just understanding them intellectually. It is about being motivated to change your present condition. But before we can do that, we need to know that our present condition isn't working or that we are suffering. We all know when we have physical suffering, but mental suffering is a bit harder to pin down. Gautama Buddha stated that there are three types of suffering, and I will briefly go through them here.

First, there is the suffering of pain. This is when we have a cold, headache, cancer or HIV, or we are sad, lonely and so on. This is easy for us to understand. This type of suffering is described as painful when it arises, painful when it remains and pleasurable when it changes.

The second one is the suffering of happiness and is a little harder to understand. Our happiness is based on causes and conditions, and so it is compounded, and anything compounded is, by its very nature, impermanent. So this happiness is not going to last, and when it ends, our suffering starts. This type of suffering is pleasurable when it arises and remains, but painful when it changes.

The final suffering is the all-pervasive suffering. This is the most difficult to understand. This type of suffering is within everything in our lives, but because it is suffering on a subtle level, we are prone to miss it. It is a condition that exists because of how we perceive ourselves in relation to the world. Our entire worldly experience is a definition of suffering that we cannot even see. We see ourselves and the world as separate—I'm here and the world is outside of me—in other words, as subject and object. We see ourselves as a solid, independent self. But Gautama Buddha taught that this is not actually the case and we are all interconnected. So the way we look at things—subject and object, me and everything else—is in some way the cause of our suffering that will come back to us in the future. This type of suffering is described as not being apparent when it arises, remains or ceases, but it is still a cause of our suffering.

Many people keep suffering because it doesn't occur to them that there may be a better way to live their lives. So once we know that we are suffering and there is another way to be, we can make a decision to try and change. That will motivate us to listen to the teachings more intently. The teachings should give you an insight into how you can change for the better. But to do this we must have confidence in the teachings and the teacher, or we are not going to be overly receptive. I am not talking about blind faith, but just a feeling that what is being said may be of help to you. Of course, once you have implemented the teachings and found, from your own experience, that they work, your trust will be based on something more solid. But at first we have to have the courage to embrace the teachings and this will make them favourable.

Don't think that every time you receive a teaching it is going to be at a favourable time. You may have to have the same teaching several times before the penny drops. I have sat through many teachings again and again, but every now and then the teacher says something that I have heard many times, but this time a light comes on in my head—I finally got the point.

So we need perseverance. If we really want a change within ourselves it is not going to come easily; it takes work. Perseverance is a skill that seems to be in short supply these days. We are so used to having things handed to us on a plate and all our communications reduced to sound bites, that we seem to lack any sense of perseverance.

So to create this favourable time we have to know we are suffering, have trust in the teachings and then be motivated, confident, patient and, above all, have perseverance. We then have to give ourselves space where we can fully engage with the teachings. Our daily review session is a good time to do this. Think about what you have heard, how it fits in with your experience of life and how you can implement it as a tool for change.

Sometimes we will go to teachings because we know the teacher will validate what we already believe. This type of teaching is not overly helpful or favourable. It is harder, and so more beneficial, to go to a teaching where you hear things that challenge your beliefs. This is because it makes you investigate what is driving you. It gives you a chance to look deeply into what your beliefs are based on. This is far more favourable than simple validation.

To finish, here are five rewards we can obtain by listening intently to the teachings. These come from the Dhammassavana Sutra:

> 'There are these five rewards in listening to the teachings. Which five? One hears what one has not heard before. One clarifies what one has heard before. One gets rid of doubt. One's views

are made straight. One's mind grows calm and stable. These are the five rewards in listening to the teachings'.

Reflection

1. Think of all the teachings you have received or read. Have they all been favourable? Why were some favourable and some not? Did you realise that all wasn't well in your life and there was a better way? Were you ready for change? Did you have trust in the teacher or teaching? Were you motivated and did you persevere?
2. What does Buddhism mean to you? Is it a badge to wear? Is it who you are or is it a mechanism to change your life? Be honest with yourself.

27—Have patience
As the saying goes, 'patience is a virtue', and it certainly is. It can also be an antidote to anger and hatred. However, it is quite difficult to be patient sometimes. When I was in my twenties it was the one thing I had very little of. I had just been promoted to manager and I had very few management skills, so I wanted things done as soon as I mentioned them; not only that, I wanted them done my way because I was manager and I knew best. I cringe now thinking about it. I used to think that people really tried my patience, until I started to follow Gautama Buddha's teachings and then I realised the problem was actually mine. There was nothing outside of me causing my impatience—it all stemmed from my own mind. The problem

wasn't what people were doing; it was they way I was reacting to what they were doing.

I had one teaching where the teacher explained a jug is filled drop by drop. That struck a chord with me, because it made me realise things are achieved slowly. Whenever I started to get impatient I would recall those words, and that helped me to calm down.

Although patience in itself is a virtue, it also shows that you have other virtues as well, such as forgiveness, tolerance and forbearance. It further shows that you have concern for other people and their views, you have compassion towards others and you have an open mind. So a lot is attached to this simple word. In the Kakacupama Sutra, Gautama Buddha gave this advice:

> '...if anyone were to reproach you right to your face, even then you should abandon those urges and thoughts which are worldly. There you should train yourself thus: "Neither shall my mind be affected by this, nor shall I give vent to evil words; but I shall remain full of concern and pity, with a mind of love, and I shall not give in to hatred." This is how you should train yourself'.

So what is patience? It is unconditionally accepting what is happening right now in the present moment. When you lack patience you are rejecting the present moment, substituting some future moment from your imagination, thinking that this future moment will help solve the imagined problem with the present moment. So we can only have patience when we are present in the moment.

Patience and the lack of it are emotions and can be worked on at a daily review session. When I looked back over my day and saw that I had been impatient, which in the early years was quite a lot, I would see that the only person who was suffering greatly was me. I was making myself agitated, tense and angry. It was only after looking closely at my impatience that I could start to let it be. Now, I cannot say my impatience has gone forever—that would be unreasonable—but I am able to catch it as it rises and then let it be.

Some people believe that by meditating we will be able to stop all of our emotions and feelings from arising. This is a common misunderstanding in Buddhism. It is impossible to stop our emotions and feelings from arising, but we can at least be aware of them when they do arise. This way we will be able to let them be and not just blindly follow them. I am going to digress a little bit here to tell you a story about stopping your emotions.

I once read a book written by a Western lama (someone who had done a three-year retreat) who was recounting the day of 9/11. He said that he was so far into his practice that he had no emotions when watching the plane fly into the tower. He didn't feel that it was good or bad. He didn't feel anything.

I am not sure I believe him. If we were able to fully stop our emotions, we would just become a cabbage. If I thought Gautama Buddha's teachings were going to do that to me, I would stop practicing straightaway. If a teacher promises you that his practice can stop your emotions, run as fast as you can. What we are looking for is an understanding of what triggers emotions and have an antidote ready for when they arrive. We have to face up to them and not try to transcend them. Emotions help us see right from wrong and pleasure from pain. By removing them we are removing a built-in value system. This value system has been built up over the years from our experiences, and even though these experiences are filtered through our view of the world, they are still a valuable tool for us to distinguish what is socially acceptable.

If we are impatient, we have to work out why that is. It is usually because we are trying to multitask, or we have set ourselves an impossibly tight schedule or we think we know better than others. We may be feeling anxious, unhappy or worried and not even know that it is because of impatience. It really does help to be aware, and your daily review session is a great tool for that. You can look for patterns and triggers, and then work on an antidote.

What we have to realise is that if we want to develop patience, we must have a change of attitude. This takes time, so at first when you start to feel impatient, try doing the three breath-calming techniques I mentioned in Chapter One. That will help you relax and let go of what is causing you to be impatient. Then start to work through your impatience at your daily review sessions.

Reflection

1. Think of the last time you were impatient. What caused it? How did you deal with it? Could you have dealt with it in a better way? What feelings did the impatience trigger? Was it the most productive way for you to act? By looking carefully at these questions we will be able to see just what a virtue patience is.

28—Giving and listening to advice
Knowing how to give and listen to advice are two skills you will need on this meandering path. You may be a seasoned practitioner and people come to you for advice. So you need to know how to advise people in a helpful and constructive way. You may be new to Gautama Buddha's teachings and ask someone for advice, so you will have to know how to listen in a way that is going to be beneficial to you. Giving and listening skills are a must.

Let's begin by looking at listening to advice. The first thing we need to understand is that there is a difference between hearing and listening. Hearing is an auditory process, whereas listening we do with our mind and heart. When we hear a sound we register it but don't necessarily engage with it. However, when we listen to something or someone we register it, give it some thought and have some opinion on it.

So listening is a much more powerful tool. Obviously, when we are listening, our views and feelings come to the surface, but don't rush into forming any opinions. Let people finish whatever they are saying. Give it a chance to sink in. It is human nature to be forming a response whilst someone is talking—resist this, as it will mean you are not fully taking on board what is being said. Stay focused. Remember what I was saying in principle 26 about sitting in a teaching but not taking it in? This was because I wasn't listening properly. Once you start doing that, your mind wanders and you end up missing what is being said.

Once you have listened to advice, ask questions if you have any doubt. If you walk away with doubt it will grow over time, so deal with it as it arises. Don't just listen to confirm what you already think. Listen to discover something new, something to shake you up and challenge your preconceptions.

A final thought: when we speak we are saying something we already know, but when we listen we may be learning something new.

Giving advice—In principle 10, right speech, I mentioned a quote from Gautama Buddha stating how to judge if our speech is right or not:

> 'It is spoken at the right time. It is spoken in truth. It is spoken affectionately. It is spoken beneficially. It is spoken with a mind of good- will'.

This applies here too. We have to be sure our advice is given at the right time; what we say is true; it is spoken in a kind and caring way; it is going to help the person; and it is not spoken out of ill will. Remember, the way you say something can make a world of difference.

Meditation/reflection and daily review sessions may bring up some difficult issues for people and they may ask your advice, but remember, you are not a therapist—know your limitations. People may be fragile and their mental state heightened, so tread carefully. They may just need to be listened to, so lend them an ear. We have to know when it is the right time to give advice and when it is time just to listen.

If someone comes to you for advice, the first thing you have to acknowledge is that you do not know everything. You should be honest. If you don't know the answer, say so. Do not lead someone down the garden path just because of your pride—be humble and truthful!

Don't judge people. The question they ask you may seem basic to you, but to them it is important or they wouldn't be asking it. Make sure your advice is given in a warm and affectionate way.

When we give advice we have to be sure we keep expectations realistic. Don't promise things you cannot deliver, such as an end to rebirth or a place in a higher realm. Make sure what you say is beneficial and not misleading.

Finally, we must never give advice when our mind is poisoned by ill will. You may have had a disagreement with this person in the past, and you now think you can get your own back by giving bad advice. This is a case where if you have nothing helpful to say, don't say anything.

Although listening to advice and giving advice may be very different things, there are similarities, the main one being that they can both be driven by ego. Once we let ego take over our listening, we are going to filter everything through our world view. This is going to stop us from truly listening, and this in turn will stop us from learning. If we let our advice stem from ego, it is going to be tinged with pride and a sense of superiority. So watch that old ego.

Reflection

1. Think back to the last time you received advice. Did you really listen? If not, what stopped you? Was it an emotion like pride, or one of the five hindrances, such as laziness? If you did listen, what were the benefits?
2. Now think about the last time you gave someone a bit of advice. Did you do it at the right time? Was it truthful and spoken with care? Was it of benefit to the other person? Did ego get in the way of you giving an unbiased response?

29—Have a teacher
Now you may be a secular Buddhist and not wish to join any group, club or organisation because you don't want to

be tied to any belief system, or you may be someone who doesn't like groups and would sooner study from books. There is no problem with either of these. However, I strongly believe you still need a teacher or mentor to help you along the meandering path.

Gautama Buddha's teachings aren't about blindly believing a set of principles or being given a practice and told to get on with it. It is about working on your own mind and experiences, sorting through your own problems and difficulties. Sometimes we are going to come across obstacles that we will need help navigating. This is where teachers come in handy. They can guide us through our difficult times and encourage us to persevere.

Even though Gautama Buddha encouraged us to be a refuge to ourselves and not look for external refuge, he wasn't talking about going it alone. He meant that we should not be looking outside of ourselves for gods or higher beings to take responsibility for our lives. That responsibility is ours and ours alone.

So a teacher is a guide, mentor and friend, not a god or higher being. Their job is to help us along the way. It states this in the *Dhammapada*, verse 276:

> 'You yourselves must strive, the masters only point the way. Those who meditate and practice the path are freed from the bonds of destructive emotions'.

There have been many reports of abuse by teachers recently, especially of a sexual nature, so it is clear we must choose our teachers very carefully. I would suggest a good teacher is someone who doesn't profess to have all the answers because that isn't possible. At the beginning of this book I said we are all in this together and we all need to do the best we can; a good teacher would be one who realises that. Good teachers are themselves simply working on their own practice and are willing to share their experiences with others. They would also be willing to learn from their students' experiences. Two necessary traits of a good teacher are humility and modesty. For our part, we should realise that teachers are only human; like us, they are flawed and will inevitably make mistakes.

Gautama Buddha did not claim any divine status for himself, nor did he say he was a personal saviour. He said he was simply a guide and teacher. So if your teachers don't have any of the characteristics mentioned above but have a title or call themselves a guru or higher being, I would suggest you check them out very carefully.

In the Anguttara Nikaya it states the five qualities we should look for in a teacher:

> 'Gautama Buddha's teachings should be taught with the thought, "I will speak step-by-step"... "I will speak explaining the sequence"..."I will speak out of compassion"..."I will speak not for the purpose of material reward"..."I will speak without disparaging others."'

Let's look at these five qualities. As we go through them, keep your teacher/mentor in mind and see if he or she embraces these five qualities.

First, the teacher should speak step by step. It is of very little use to learn about emptiness or nonself if you haven't first understood that there is an unease or discontentment running through your life. When I first started studying Buddhism I had so many teachings on what a Bodhisattva does and doesn't do, but I didn't know exactly what I was supposed to be doing myself. I learnt about how Milarepa (a famous Tibetan yogi) became enlightened in one lifetime, but Gautama Buddha took three countless aeons. I expect these stories have their place, but it certainly isn't when one is just starting out on the path.

We need to start at the beginning of the path and slowly work our way along, one step at a time. This will help reduce any confusion. Many students get so confused that they turn away from Buddhism, believing it is not relevant to them, when in fact it could be the teacher's fault for not teaching step by step. One of the great things about Buddhism is that Gautama Buddha's discourses are numbered—five precepts, ten harmful acts, four truths, five qualities of a teacher—which makes it easier to follow and remember the individual steps of the teachings.

Second, the teacher should explain the sequence. I have had teachings where someone has asked about why are things done in this order, only to be told that it is tradition—very annoying and not very helpful. So the sequence should be explained. Why in the four truths do we start with 'there is suffering' and then go on to 'the causes of suffering', followed by 'there is an end, or at least a way to reduce, suffering', and finally, 'the path that leads to the reduction of our suffering'? There is a reason for this sequence and your teacher should explain it clearly. This will ensure there is no confusion or misunderstanding.

Third, the teacher's motivation for teaching should be one of kindness, caring and compassion. Teachers should see that people are discontented with their lives and need some help to find their way. Teachers should not be motivated by pride, thinking they are better than their students, or arrogant, thinking they know more than their students. Their teachings should be grounded in an overwhelming sense of wanting to help others.

Fourth, the teacher should not teach just to get material gain. In Tibetan Buddhism (and probably other forms of Buddhism as well, but I only have experience of Tibetan Buddhist teachers) many teachers have huge houses, large cars, big TVs and all the material trappings of the twenty-first century—all paid for by their students. This really is a turnoff. How can you sit and listen to a teacher telling you not to get attached to things when the teacher quite clearly is attached to them? This goes back to a point I mentioned earlier: teachers' words should reflect their actions. It is stated in Tibetan Buddhism that all teachers are such realised beings that they are above any sort of attachment, so they can drink alcohol, smoke, eat meat— pretty much do whatever they want to do. Now, isn't that convenient? It seems to ignore the fact that the teacher is a human being and so subject to the same feelings and emotions as everybody else. Of course, some teachers have reached a point where they can focus on positive emotions and feelings and let the negative ones be. However, this is a rarity and not, as Tibetan Buddhism leads you to believe, the norm.

I understand that some teachers are professionals and have to charge to make a living. I have no problem with that as long as their fees are reasonable and they are not just teaching to rip people off. A friend of mine told me a story about when she went to a teaching in America. She wasn't working at the time and so had very little money, but she really wanted the teaching. She asked the centre if she could do some work for them to pay off the cost of the teaching. She was told that it wasn't a charity. She would never go to a supermarket and ask to work to pay off her grocery bill, so why is she asking here? This is wrong on so many levels.

Finally, their teachings should not disparage others. I have to be honest with you and say I have had quite a few teachings that have put other schools of Buddhism down. This, I believe, is done so teachers can gain control over their students. They say that their teachings are the quickest, best, simplest, most powerful way to reach enlightenment—all of this is said without offering any proof.

I have also had teachers make fun of other religions because these don't believe what Buddhists believe. One ridiculed other religions for believing in god, and then he proceeded to do a protector prayer. This prayer is to ask some mythical being outside of yourself to help you—in other words, a god.

Gautama Buddha's teachings are just one form of help we can use to improve our lives, but they clearly aren't the only one. We are all different, and so what suits one will not suit another. So the teacher should give you the facts and not spend time disparaging others.

I would like to add another quality that I think is very important, and that is the five precepts. I believe any Buddhist teacher should attempt to follow the precepts. Of course they are only human and may come up short sometimes, but they should at least try to follow them. I find it hard to take teachings on board when teachers are trying to teach me how to act, and they quite clearly cannot act that way themselves. 'Do as I say and not as I do' doesn't work these days. In the Cunda Sutra, Gautama Buddha stated this about someone who proclaims to know his teachings, but whose actions do not match his words:

> 'When a venerable one utters words about knowing...about developing...about knowing and developing, saying, "I know this teaching; I see this teaching; I am developed in bodily action, developed in virtue, developed in mind, developed in discernment," but he remains with his mind conquered by greed, his mind conquered by aversion, delusion, anger, hostility, hypocrisy, spite, selfishness, envy, or longing, then it should

be known of him that, "This venerable one does not discern how it is that, when one discerns, greed does not come into being, which is why he remains with his mind conquered by greed. This venerable one does not discern how it is that, when one discerns aversion...delusion...anger...hostility...hypocrisy...spite...selfishness...envy...longing does not come into being, which is why he remains with his mind conquered by evil longing."'

Check your teachers carefully and be sure their words and actions match. Also be sure your teachers challenge you and not just make you feel comfortable and safe.

How should the student act? Some people think to show respect to their teachers they have to bow down to them, treat them as higher beings, shower them with gifts and blindly follow every word they say. I do not think this sycophantic way of acting is giving respect. If you truly want to respect your teachers, then listen to their teachings, ask questions to clear up any doubts, reflect and meditate on the teaching and then, finally, put what they have taught into practice. What better way to respect anyone?

The problem with students acting this way is that they sometimes end up lusting after time with teachers, hanging on their every word and doing things they wouldn't usually do just to please this higher being. They totally forget that this is about the student, not the teacher. They project special powers onto teachers, which they don't have. I have a friend who thinks his teacher can hear and see everything that is happening to his students. If the teacher looks at him in an angry way, he will look back over the last few days and imagine it is for something he did. This way of thinking is not just irrational, it is also dangerous, as it is leaving you wide open for abuse and a big fall.

Once you start seeing this human being as someone higher, better, and more worthy than yourself, you start along that slippery slope of being taken for a ride. This is how cults are formed. You think the teacher is a godlike figure who knows what is good for you, so you surrender. He gets you doing irrational and quite often immoral things, but you blindly follow because he is the chosen one, he knows best. This can lead you to act in an unethical way, do things you would never have dreamed of doing until you met your teacher, and it can also lead to psychological problems. What it definitely won't do is help alleviate your suffering.

I think you have to look carefully at what you want out of your relationship with your teacher. You can do this in one of your daily review sessions. Do you want a guide to help you reduce your suffering, or do you want someone to take responsibility for your life? 'Are you wanting to learn from them or lean on them?'

Gautama Buddha's teachings are an inward journey where we look at the human condition and try to tweak it to make life more bearable. It isn't about handing over your life to someone else and letting them do whatever they want with it. I believe it is a journey of discovery about what makes us who we are, why we act in a certain way and how we can reduce the suffering in our life. For me it is not about mythical figures or realms; I see those as the outside world. It is about trying to make myself the best possible person I can be in this life, and that is why I need a teacher, or teachers, to help me explore my inner world. I don't want to lean on them—I have my friends for that—I want to learn from them.

If your teachers are any good they will tell you up front they do not have all the answers, they are not a higher being and they are just sharing their experiences and want to learn from your experiences. But many teachers love the adulation as it boosts their pride and makes them feel special. For them it is all about ego, power, control and money; it has very little to do with wanting to help others.

I will end on a positive note. There are without doubt some wonderful teachers out there who are compassionate, grounded and informed; we just have to find them. I will reiterate what I said at the start of this principle: it is extremely important to have a teacher/mentor to guide us along our chosen path, so please do not be put off by bad teachers—good teachers by far outweigh the bad ones.

Reflection

1. Do your teachers have the five qualities mentioned above? Do their actions match their words? Do their students' actions match their teachings? It is up to you to check.

2. Do you project qualities onto your teachers that just aren't there? Do you treat them as a higher being? Why is that? Are you looking for someone to take responsibility for your life? Are you a learner or a leaner?
3. Think about what you are looking for in a teacher. What is it you want out of the relationship? Are you getting it? If not, why are you still there?

30—Discuss the teachings

The main reasons for discussing the teachings is to clear up any doubts you may have, prevent you from just blindly following what has been said and to help you with your understanding of the teaching.

Doubt was mentioned in Chapter One under the five hindrances because it can totally take you off course, stop you from implementing the teaching and cause you to walk away thinking this teaching is not for you. I know in many traditional texts it is stated that you should not have doubt. But how is that possible? If you have doubt, then you have doubt. Doubts are not going to be cleared up by saying you shouldn't have them.

What these traditional texts want you to do is blindly follow the teachings and the teachers. In my experience, this doesn't work. If I have doubts I discuss them and try to clear them up. I don't suppress them or pretend I don't have doubts. In the Magandiya Sutra, Gautama Buddha told a story about a blind man and a piece of white cloth, which shows how unhelpful blind faith is.

There was this man who was blind from birth who had heard from people with good eyesight that a piece of white cloth was beautiful, spotless and clean. So he went in search of a piece of white cloth. He came upon a man who said he had a beautiful, spotless, clean piece of white cloth, but what he actually had was a grimy, oil-stained rag. The blind man took the rag and put it on. He though he had a piece of white cloth, so he was gratified. Gautama Buddha asked the assembly if the blind man had taken the cloth out of faith or through knowing and seeing. Of course they proclaimed it was out of faith, and Gautama Buddha said we should never accept things out of faith alone. We should only accept things from knowing and seeing, which means from our experience.

So don't blindly believe things; check to see if they fit your experiences. We have to listen to, or read, teachings with a critical mind. It doesn't matter if the book you are reading is a hundred-or-so years old, or your teacher has a wonderful title; we still need to check out what is being said. That goes for this book as well—check it out and see if it fits with your experiences, please don't blindly believe it.

The final point here is that we need to discuss the teachings in order to help with our understanding. It is great to have a group of like-minded people to bounce things off or a friend that is also following the teachings of Gautama Buddha. Whilst writing this and my previous book, I had many in-depth conversations with a friend of mine. We had been to many of the same teachings, but had in some cases interpreted the teachings slightly differently. It is funny, but once you start to articulate things they can seem different to how you imagined them in your head.

If you are studying in a group, don't be afraid to raise any doubts you may have. When I first started studying Gautama Buddha's teachings I found it hard to believe in rebirth—I think a lot of Westerners struggle with this concept. As I was in a group I didn't want to bring it up because I thought everyone else believed it. It became quite an obstacle for me and was starting to prevent me from moving forward with my studies. So one day I brought it up in a question-and-answer session. To my surprise, over eighty percent of the group were also struggling with it. It was such a weight off my shoulders.

My teacher at the time was quite forward thinking and told us not to worry about it, leave it to one side and and move on. He advised us to revisit the issue now and again and see if it had started to fit into place. I have to say that it never has with me, but it hasn't stopped my studies or, more important, my practice. As I have previously stated, I don't know if I have been here before or if I will visit again, but what I do know is that I am here now, and that is what is most important to me. We have to understand that sometimes issues, such as rebirth or the traditional understanding of karma, cannot be reconciled, so don't worry. It is fine to put things on the back burner. What we shouldn't do is throw Buddha out with the bath water by dismissing the whole of his teachings because of these things.

Reflection

1. Do you have doubts? Are they making obstacles for you? If so, why are you not discussing them?

You can think over the doubts you may have in a daily review session. Make a list of blockages and find a teacher or spiritual friend to discuss them with. Slowly work through the list, and then move on along this meandering path.

Summary
These are the individual principles we should try to follow. We should be humble, grateful and patient, as this will benefit ourselves as well as others. We should also be content with what we have, because if we are, we will always have enough. Someone once told me that it is not about being rich, but about being contented—great advice.

We need to have teachings at a favourable time. Find a good teacher and discuss the teachings to stop any doubt. We also need to learn how to give and listen to advice. Finally, we should be willing to show respect to people who have helped us.

In your daily review sessions look to see if you are humble or proud, grateful or thankless, patient or inpatient, contented or unsatisfied. Work on building good qualities and reducing the unhelpful ones.

8
Refining Principles

WE HAVE NOW come to the final set of principles and put the roof on the house we have been building.

The refining principles are where we improve on and perfect the principles that have gone before. Here we look at how we can practice self-restraint, understand why we are suffering and what path we can take to reduce that suffering. We will look at some of Gautama Buddha's most important teachings, such as impermanence, nonself and defilements.

There is a lot to cover and take on board in this chapter, so please go through it slowly. It is not a race and there are no prizes or awards for the one who gets through it the quickest. Keep in mind that it is your personal journey, and so the speed of another person has no bearing on your progress; only you can determine if you are ready to move onto the next principle or not.

31—Practice self-restraint

Throughout this book I have mentioned that all of our actions of body and speech stem from our mind, so it is vitally important to have a strategy whereby we can have some self-restraint over our thoughts, feelings and emotions. I am not saying we have to try and control or suppress them, just get in tune with them. Mindfulness is one way of doing this. A lot of people believe mindfulness can only be achieved on the meditation cushion. This is not correct. Although we do mindfulness meditation practices, we have to take the insights we gain from that and introduce them into our daily lives. If we are extremely mindful on our cushion, but when we go outside we are driven by thoughts of the past or the future, what is the point of our mindfulness practice?

We have to remain focused on the task at hand, and not let our minds wander off to the future or float back to the past. When we are walking we should be fully aware that we are walking. When we are eating, sitting, washing, talking, listening and so on, we should be fully in tune with what we are doing and what is happening around us. This way of being will enable us to watch our thoughts, feelings and emotions as they arise, so we can weed out the unhelpful ones and allow only the helpful ones to materialise into actions of body and speech.

So often we just do and say things out of habit. Even though they have not served us well in the past, we still do them. We are trapped in our comfort zone. So what we need to do is become aware of our thoughts before they turn into actions. If you are not convinced that your thoughts control your feelings, emotions and actions, just try feeling unhappy without having unhappy or negative thoughts—it cannot be done. This is the same for happiness, anger, sadness, pride, jealousy and so on. In order to experience any feeling or emotion, you have to first have the thought that produces it. The same goes for any action; first we think we are going to walk, and then we walk. It is the same for our speech. We don't just tell a lie; we have the thought that we are going to lie, and then we lie. This is how important our thoughts are. Some people say, 'Oh! Sorry that just came out', but it wouldn't have if they had been mindful.

If we check to see if what we are about to do or say is going to be helpful or harmful, we will be able to restrain from the harmful and concentrate on the helpful. You can also look at your actions during your daily review and see what worked and what didn't, and next time you are in the situation where something didn't work, remain mindful and act in a more helpful way.

Another very good way to train ourselves in self-restraint, and being able to stay focused, is to have a day of observance. This is when you make a promise to yourself to observe the eight precepts. You can observe them for one day, a week, a month, a year or even for the rest of your life. However, most people would do them for a day because they have family or work commitments. It is possible to do them for a longer period if you attend an organised retreat. A lot of people will wait for a certain day or date to have a day of observance, but I believe it is not necessary to wait for a special day, such as a new or full moon day. A good day to choose is when you are not working, so you can concentrate on doing practice, reading books or listening to teachings of Gautama Buddha. I would suggest you try to do a day of observance once a week, but at the very least once a month.

These precepts are the five precepts, as mentioned in principle 9, with an extra three precepts:

- Refrain from killing
- Refrain from stealing
- Refrain from wrong speech
- Refrain from sexual misconduct
- Refrain from intoxicants and illegal drugs
- Refrain from eating at the wrong time
- Refrain from any type of entertainment and from beautifying yourself
- Refrain from sleeping on a luxurious bed

On the day of observance you should rise at dawn and make a commitment to adhere to the eight precepts until dawn the next day. You do not have to make the promise to a god or your teacher or anyone else; just make it to yourself because it is you who is going to benefit, and it is also you who will be cheated if you do not carry out the observance.

Precept one is refrain from killing, and so it is good not to eat any meat on this day and to remain conscious of not killing any animals or insects. For the first five precepts, go back to principle 9 and reread that section as a reminder of what you are required to refrain from.

Precept two is refrain from stealing, so do not take what has not been given.

Precept three is refrain from wrong speech and If you come into contact with others on this day, be sure you think before you speak. Do not say anything until you have checked to see if it is true, helpful and kind. I believe it is much better to take a vow of silence on this day. It has two benefits: you do not have to worry about wrong speech and, most important, you remain totally focused as there is just you and your thoughts and that is a very powerful combination.

Precept four is refrain from sexual misconduct, so do not engage in any sexual activities on this day. That means no sex between dawn one day and dawn the next day. This is not saying that sex is a bad thing, only that it is a distraction and something we get attached to, so it is better to refrain from it for one day.

Precept five is refrain from intoxicants and illegal drugs, and we should not take any intoxicants on this day. Of course, medicinal drugs are permitted.

Precept six concerns not eating at the wrong time, and so we should not eat and drink after noon on the day of observance. It is advisable to eat and drink at around eleven thirty in the morning and then not to eat or drink anything after that until dawn the next day. I would suggest that if you live in a hot country, you should take a sip of water periodically throughout the day, but refrain from drinking anything else.

This is not a form of punishment or penance; it is to help you remain focused on your practice, especially meditation practice. When we have eaten a meal it makes us feel heavy and sluggish, and both of these are not helpful for meditation as they make you feel sleepy. I would advise you not to eat twice as much at eleven thirty, hoping it will see you through till dawn, as this does not work—I know because I tried it. It will only make you feel bloated and uncomfortable.

Remember, if you lose your self-restraint and take a bite to eat or have a drink between noon and dawn, don't be hard on yourself. Just retake the precept and focus your attention back on your practice.

Precept seven is divided into two parts; refraining from entertainment and beautifying oneself.

The first part is aimed at keeping your mind, body and speech away from all kinds of entertainment. Not, of course, that they are "sinful," but that they disturb our mind and excite the senses. This covers TV, radio, cinema, sporting events and even the Internet. I would further suggest you turn off your phone from dawn until dawn the next day—I know some of you will be horrified by that thought, but don't worry, the world won't end.

The second part covers not wearing makeup, jewellery and perfumes. This is to stop any form of vanity and conceitedness from arising. It also takes you back to basics. It doesn't matter what your hair looks like or if your clothes are nicely ironed. What matters is that you stay focused on your practice and train yourself in self-restraint.

Precept eight covers not sleeping on a luxurious bed. Throughout the day you have cut out other luxuries, so the luxury of a large, soft bed should also be dispensed with. You could put a mattress on the floor or sleep on your own in the spare room. This is not for punishment, but to help build your self-restraint.

I have heard of people going to bed at six in the evening because they were hungry and couldn't watch the telly, so they thought they would sleep and when they wake up, they can eat and get back to their normal way of life. This is missing the point. Use your free time to study, reflect, and do your practice.

So these are the eight precepts to follow during your day of observance. They are meant to build your mental and bodily discipline and are not a penance. If you fall short on any of these precepts during the day, don't beat yourself up; just retake the precept and move on.

Setting up a day of observance takes planning. You have to be sure that your family and friends know what you are doing so they don't disturb you. The first time may be a bit hit-and-miss, but don't give up. The rewards are worth it, and in the end it will help build your self-restraint and make your life much simpler.

In the *Dhammapada*, verse 234, it states this:

> 'The wise who restrain their body, who restrain their tongue, the wise who restrain their mind, are indeed well restrained'.

Reflection

1. Are you mindful of your actions? Do you ever say or do something without first checking to see if it is helpful or harmful? Think what it would be like to practice self-restraint. Do you think you could do it? What would stop you? Work through any obstacles you feel you may have.

I would strongly encourage you to do a day of observance before you move on. If that isn't possible, at the very least set a date for one. It will help you along this meandering path greatly.

32—Understand the four truths

Gautama Buddha's first teaching was on the four truths, which showed us that we are suffering, there are causes of this suffering, there is an end to suffering, and finally, there is a path to follow to bring the suffering to an end. This discourse was one of his most important as it encompasses the whole of his teachings. In the Hatthipadopama Sutra, one of Gautama Buddha's chief disciples, Sariputta, said:

> 'Friends, just as the footprints of all legged animals are encompassed by the footprint of the elephant, and the elephant's footprint is reckoned the foremost among them in terms of size, in the same way, all skilful qualities are gathered under the Four Truths'.

There are three points I would like to cover here before we discuss each of the truths individually. First, I am not convinced that we can totally end our suffering, but I do strongly believe we can significantly reduce it or, at the very least, manage our expectations better. Second, these four truths are best understood not as beliefs, but as categories of experience. So please do not dismiss them as a belief system or as being too basic. Both of these are totally incorrect. Third, I want to remind you about what I said concerning the meaning of suffering. In Gautama Buddha's teachings the word used is *dukkha*, which is commonly translated as suffering. The suffering we are talking about isn't just physical pain, but also emotional torment.

It includes a feeling of dissatisfaction, anxiety, anguish, unhappiness, desire, discontent, unease, a feeling of not being whole, frustration and even depression. The list could go on, but I think you get the picture. So whenever I use the word suffering I am using it as an umbrella term to cover all of the above.

Many people say that Gautama Buddha was being pessimistic when he taught the four truths because they are about suffering. I don't believe this charge is correct. The first truth is a diagnosis of the problems facing us, so you could liken Gautama Buddha to a doctor. In the second truth he points out the causes of the suffering. He then goes on to inform us there is a cure, and finally in the fourth truth, he tells us what we need to do to cure our problem. So saying he was pessimistic is like saying a doctor is being pessimistic when he asks you, 'Where is your pain?' Gautama Buddha's teachings were neither pessimistic nor optimistic; they were actually realistic.

The first discourse, which covered the four truths, was called the Dhammacakkappavattana Sutra. Here is a stanza from that sutra that states we should steer clear of the two extremes:

> 'There are these two extremes that are not to be indulged in by one who has gone forth. Which two? That which is devoted to sensual pleasure with reference to sensual objects: base, vulgar,

common, ignoble, unprofitable; and that which is devoted to self-affliction: painful, ignoble, unprofitable. Avoiding both of these extremes is known as the middle way'.

The first of the two extremes we should try not to indulge in is sense objects, such as sight, sound, smell, taste and touch. If we get too caught up in such pleasures, both physically and mentally, we start to chase after them and eventually we cannot think of anything else.

We have all, at one time or another, seen something new and thought, 'I really need that, I can't live without it, I really must have it at any cost'. It consumes all of our thoughts and we even dream about it at night. This kind of attachment is what Gautama Buddha was warning us against in this extreme.

He wasn't saying that we shouldn't have any pleasure or happiness in our lives—that would just be another extreme—but only that we should not get ourselves completely entangled with objects of the senses.

When we get so attached to things we start holding on to them and have feelings of pride because we have this great new gadget, or else jealousy arises because someone else has it and we cannot afford it.

These sense objects can never bring us real and lasting happiness; they bring just brief moments of enjoyment that will soon pass. When they're gone, they leave a feeling of discontentment, frustration and misery. This is the suffering we are talking about here.

There is no doubt we should try and enjoy ourselves, but we have to understand that enjoyment is fleeting and will not release us from the suffering we feel in our lives. If we enjoy ourselves while keeping this in mind, we will enjoy with wisdom and not blindly.

The second extreme to be avoided is self-mortification or self-destructive behaviour.

In the time of Gautama Buddha, some religious people in India put themselves through tremendous pain and torture. All this achieved was more suffering. It was not uncommon during this time for religious people to starve themselves, plunge into freezing water in the middle of winter, stand completely naked under the blistering heat in the height of the summer, and even sleep on beds of thorns. They believed by torturing their bodies in this way they could purify bad karma from past lives.

Today we can see many people in a self-destructive mode: people who smoke cigarettes or drugs, drink too much alcohol, take illegal drugs or are addicted to gambling. All of these put you on a path that can lead to harming yourself.

Even though there is a wealth of medical evidence concerning the damage to your health because of smoking, drinking alcohol and the taking illegal drugs, people still indulge in them. It is as if they don't care what damage they are doing to themselves. This is self-destructive behaviour.

Some people are addicted to gambling. Even though they have very little money, they would rather gamble it away than buy food, clothes or spend it on supporting their family. This again is destructive behaviour.

The way we abuse our bodies may have changed since Gautama Buddha's time, but the consequences of the actions remain the same. We should avoid extreme behaviour.

Our lives are precious and should be looked after. If you have an able body and all of your faculties, you should rejoice and use them to help others who are less fortunate. What we shouldn't do is torture our body or end our life prematurely by setting ourselves on fire or going on a hunger strike because of some disagreement or other. You may hit the headlines for a day or two, but after that the world moves on and you are forgotten—now, tell me that isn't a waste of your life.

When Gautama Buddha cautioned us against doing such things, he was talking from experience. When he was young he had a very privileged upbringing, which is where he experienced the first extreme. Once he left his home, he spent six years doing austere practices mentioned in the second extreme. In fact he nearly starved himself to death, but realised in time that this form of self-torture will not reduce his suffering; it will only increase it.

These extremes are two different sides of the same coin. They both spring from unawareness and lead to suffering. They will never remove the feelings of discontent and unease in our lives. We have to tread the middle ground between these two extremes.

Reflection

1. Think of the last material thing you bought. Did it make you happy? Did that happiness last? Are you now craving something else to make you happy? Have you found lasting happiness or are you constantly chasing after it?
2. Do you think self-destructive behaviour will help reduce your suffering? Do you think by putting yourself through excruciating pain it will somehow reduce the pain in your life?

First truth—the truth of suffering
Gautama Buddha spoke about three different types of suffering, which were explained in principle 26.

But let us do a quick recap. We can clearly understand the first type of suffering, as it is suffering on a day-to-day basis, such as when we are sick, sad, hungry, lonely or cold. But the second suffering, the suffering of happiness, is harder for us to grasp. When things break, end or die, which they inevitably will, it brings us tremendous suffering because we had grown attached to them. So the happiness has turned into a form of suffering. In the third type of suffering we see the world in a dualistic way; I am here and the world is outside of me—subject and object. This way of thinking brings us suffering because we divide things into like and dislike, which in turn makes us become attached to certain things and repelled by others. This causes us to split the world into me and others and is a constant cause of our suffering. This is briefly the three types of suffering Gautama Buddha spoke about.

Let's look at the stanza explaining the first truth in more detail:

> 'This is the truth of suffering: Birth is suffering, ageing is suffering, death is suffering; sorrow, lamentation, pain, distress and despair are suffering; being associated with what one dislikes is suffering, being separated from what one likes is suffering, not getting what is wanted is suffering'.

In the above stanza Gautama Buddha stated that birth, ageing and death are all a distinct feature of life that bring us suffering.

Birth can be extremely painful, not just for mothers, but also for babies who are trying to make sense of the world they suddenly find themselves in. They cannot communicate what they want or what they are feeling, so they get frustrated and cry. Everything around them is alien and scary. They have to adapt to this world, and that causes them to get frustrated and feel frightened.

Old age usually brings on illness, pain and sometimes loneliness, and eventually death. As we grow older our body starts to wear out. Things we once enjoyed we can no longer do. Our joints, eyesight and hearing start to fail us. Our friends start dying and we become frustrated and lonely. Inside we know we are heading towards death, but we are too frightened to face it. Death is ever present; it feels like an albatross around our necks. Old age for many people is a difficult and sad time.

Life can fill us with sadness, lamentation, pain, distress, and despair. These are all reactions to losing the things we love and are attached to. Everything is compounded and subject to change, so no matter what we get attached to, it will eventually bring us suffering.

Just imagine you have been saving for years to get the car of your dreams. You eventually have enough money to buy it, and the day you drive it out of the garage you are filled with elation. But after a while someone steals the car and you are left with a feeling of sorrow, lamentation and despair. The happiness you had a few weeks ago has now turned to suffering. This happens to all things we get attached to. I can remember, before I was a monk, buying a new Range Rover, and the very first day I drove it, someone ran into the back of it. It instantly took the shine off of having a new car, and my inevitable suffering began.

Being associated with what one dislikes makes us dissatisfied, which is a form of suffering. Maybe your partner's friends are not your cup of tea, but because you love your partner, you associate with these friends even though it makes you irritable and unhappy. Sometimes through work we have to associate with people we dislike and this makes us uncomfortable, and so we suffer. When I worked in London, part of my job was to have dinner with other people from my industry. I used to dread this because I had very little in common with these people, and so found it hard to associate with them. It caused me endless suffering.

We should bear in mind that these are just our projections; our dislike is not inherent in the other person. This understanding will help reduce your suffering, but will not totally end it.

Being separated from what one likes causes us to suffer. When we are not with the people we love, be it our partner, friends or family, we feel sad and anxious. Also, not being surrounded by the material things we like because they are broken or stolen brings us pain. The material thing doesn't have to be lost, maybe it just isn't working, but we still suffer. I know when I go somewhere and I don't have a signal on my phone or the Internet connection isn't working, I get irritable and annoyed. A simple thing like this can cause us so much suffering.

Not getting what one wants causes us suffering. We all have hopes, dreams and desires, but these do not always come to fruition. We cannot always do the things we want to do or own the things we crave for, so we try to make the best of things. But deep inside we are tormented by disappointment and discontent. Instead of being able to purchase the car of your dreams, you have to make do with a cheaper model. Although the car still gets you from A to B, you are not satisfied and so suffer. Maybe you are not in the profession you would really like to be in, but you have to make do with a lesser job because it pays the rent. This again will make you dissatisfied and suffer. I am sure we can all think of stories where we didn't get what we wanted, and so we suffered. I know when I was a child I threw endless tantrums because I didn't get what I wanted; this was my own personal suffering.

So what Gautama Buddha was saying in the stanza above was that everything that takes place on a day-to-day basis can cause us to suffer. Now we must be clear that he said there is suffering, and not you are suffering. He didn't explain there is suffering so you can identify with the problem. The common bond we share with all beings is suffering; it is the thread that runs through all our lives. He explained the truth of suffering for you to simply acknowledge that there is a problem. This is the first important step towards reducing our suffering.

He wanted us to witness our suffering and to fully understand it. If you do not understand that there is suffering in your life and that it is causing you a problem, you will not be motivated to alleviate it. So he made it clear in his first truth that there is endless suffering in our lives.

Reflection

1. Think about your life. Does the mere fact that you are alive cause you to suffer? Does being associated with what you dislike cause you to suffer? Does being separated from what you like cause you to suffer? Does not getting what you want cause you to suffer? Can you relate to the three types of suffering?

As I have stated above, it is extremely important to understand there is suffering in your life. So look at the reflections carefully and be sure you have managed to get in touch with your suffering. This isn't to depress you; it will allow you to move on to the next truth. We cannot deal with something if we do not know we have it. If your illness lies undetected, you cannot start to deal with it, and if your suffering lies undetected, you cannot start the process of dealing with it. So connect with your suffering before you move on.

Second truth—the causes of suffering

As you can see from above, suffering is running throughout everything we do in our lives. Because of that fact, there is not just one cause of our suffering, as there is not one cause of anything. Things come into being through a series of causes and conditions, and that is the same for our suffering. However, there are three main things that cause us interminable suffering, namely, the three poisons. They are clinging desire, anger and aversion and unawareness.

In the *Dhammapada* it states:

> 'The one who protects his mind from clinging desire, anger and aversion and unawareness, is the one who enjoys real and lasting peace'.

Let's take a look at the poisons that are making us suffer.

Clinging Desire
Not all of our desires cause us suffering; only the ones we cling to. We may have a desire to help people, a desire to reduce our suffering or to improve ourselves. As long as we are not clinging to these desires there is no problem. In the Sacitta Sutra, Gautama Buddha stated that if we have unhelpful qualities, we should put forth extra desire to change them. He likened it to a person whose head is on fire:

> 'If, on examination, a person knows, "I usually remain covetous, with thoughts of ill will, overcome by sloth and drowsiness, restless, uncertain, angry, with harmful thoughts, with my body aroused, lazy or not concentrated," then he should *put forth extra desire*, effort, diligence, endeavour, relentlessness, mindfulness and alertness for the abandoning of those very same unhelpful qualities. Just as when a person whose head was on fire would *put forth extra desire*, effort, diligence, endeavour, relentlessness, mindfulness and alertness to put out the fire on his head'.

So desire on its own isn't the problem. The problem is our clinging and grasping at the things we desire. We wrongly believe that material things and people, such as family, friends and loved ones, can make us permanently and truly happy. However, if we take the time to investigate, we will find that these desires eventually lead us into a feeling of discontentment, sadness and loss. Why is that? It is because we have grown attached to the people we love or the things we own. Again, there is not a problem with loving the people close to us; the suffering starts once we get attached to them, believe they will be with us forever and their thoughts and feelings for us will never change. This simply isn't the case.

You can test this theory out. Think of a time when someone not very close to you died. How did you feel? I expect you expressed your condolences, but didn't have too much sadness. Now think of a time when a member of your family, a friend or a loved one died. How did you feel? I expect you were devastated and extremely upset for a long time. So what is the difference between these two deaths? Attachment. You were not attached to the first person and so did not suffer a lot when they died, but you were attached to the second person, and your clinging attachment is what caused you so much suffering.

We get attached to our belongings and believe they make us happy. We think we can buy happiness. The problem with that is our desires are never ending. Once we have something new, we start wanting something else. We never quite manage to buy the happiness we are so desperately seeking because there is no happiness inherent in material things. We just project happiness onto an object and then cling and grasp at this imaginary happiness, and we eventually suffer once the object is stolen or stops working.

I have to stress the point that there is no problem in wanting things and trying to make our lives more comfortable; the problem is clinging and grasping at these desires. So do not stop loving the people close to you or stop wanting to improve your life believing Gautama Buddha told us to do that—it simply isn't true.

Our clinging desires lead us to act in certain ways, such as being proud, jealous and protective, and this in turn leads to our discontentment. This is because our clinging desires lead us into action, which in turn leads us into discontentment. It is a vicious cycle. In the Itivuttaka, Gautama Buddha said:

> 'From desire action follows; from action discontentment follows; desire, action and discontentment are like a wheel rotating endlessly'.

To break this cycle, we have to see that clinging, grasping and getting attached to people and material objects brings us suffering because things are compounded and are subject to change. If we can truly embrace this point and apply it to our daily lives, we will be able to reduce the suffering caused by this poison.

Finally, the Iccha Sutra states:

> 'With clinging desire the world is tied down. With the subduing of clinging desire it's freed. With the abandoning of clinging desire all bonds are cut through'.

Reflection

1. Think of something or someone that you desire at the moment; look at your desire deeply. Are you clinging to that desire? Does it inherently have happiness in it? Is it going to bring you lasting happiness? Do you believe it will eventually change? If so, why are you clinging to it? Would it not bring you less suffering if you saw it as a brief moment of pleasure that will change in the future?

Anger and Aversion

Aversion is when we dislike something and push it away; it is the opposite of attachment. Anger leads to hatred, discrimination, aggression and a lack of compassion. None of these is a helpful emotion.

With desire we want to cling to objects, but with aversion we do the exact opposite. When we see something we dislike, instantly our aversion arises. When this happens we need to let it be, not engage with it, as engaging with it reinforces the aversion. Do not try to repress it or, out of a sense of shame, pretend it isn't there; acknowledge it and let it be. This takes practice, and so a good time to work on your aversion is in your daily review sessions. Look truthfully at the things that cause your aversion to rise and work out a strategy to deal with them. Then when they start to arise you can spot them and just let them be. When I say 'let them be' I mean do not engage them or push them away; let them be and they will disappear. Some people say let them go, but to me that is an action and so you are engaging with them. By letting them be you are not engaging in any way.

Maybe we have an aversion to a certain type of person. I know when I was young we were told the Russians were bad people, and these days we are told it is the Muslims. This is us being conditioned to have aversion. It is totally irrational, but if we don't let the aversion be, it will grow stronger and more destructive. This aversion can drive us to make adverse comments about these people, and when we see them, a strong feeling of dislike and mistrust arises within us. However, if we spend time and examine these feelings, we will see that there is no reason for us to feel this way. By examining our aversion for these people in our daily review, we will be able to eventually let the aversion be, as we will see that these people are actually just like us: they do not want to suffer and they want to try to be happy. So it makes no sense to have any aversion towards them. If we begin to think like this, compassion will start to arise in us and we will slowly start to lose any aversion we have for them.

If we do not spend time looking at our aversions and start to acknowledge them, we are likely to fall into denial, which is not good for our state of mind. So train yourself to watch the aversion rise and fall—do not engage with it. Just work at letting it be. It takes time, but once we can start letting the aversion be it will no longer make us suffer.

In the Kodhana Sutra, Gautama Buddha said this about anger:

> 'This fury does so cloud the mind of man that he cannot discern this fearful inner danger'.

Anger is one of the most destructive emotions because we engage with it and let it control our thoughts, feelings and actions. Anger makes us uninhibited. People usually think that there is only two ways of dealing with anger: express or repress. Both of these are unhealthy. Some say that anger is natural and should be expressed. If you express it, it can lead to acting in a violent way, it can cause hatred and we can end up saying and doing things that harm others. In a worst-case scenario, it can lead to war and acts of terrorism. If you repress it, all you are doing is storing up trouble for the future. You may be able to keep it down for some time, but eventually it will surface and may even come back more violent and more harmful. It could also lead to health issues.

I feel anger should not be dismissed as just something that is natural. Anger arises out of jealousy, pride, frustration, tiredness or a deep-rooted irrational prejudice. We may see a certain type of person that we dislike because they look, dress, talk or act differently than we do. We start projecting negative qualities onto these people, and this makes us feel angry.

The feelings and emotions that produce our anger may arise naturally, but we do not have to choose to blindly follow them. Even if you still strongly believe anger is natural, it doesn't follow that it is beneficial to us or the person with whom we are angry.

Gautama Buddha thought expressing or repressing our anger was just going to lead to more suffering for ourselves and others, so he advised us to look at the anger and see where it came from. This you can do in your daily review. Look back on your anger, see how you could have acted more calmly, and imagine what the outcome may have been if you had. Slowly, you will learn not to react instantly but to first reflect.

We have to understand that anger is not to be dealt with, but simply observed and let be. If we observe it, we will see that it stems from our exaggerating the negative qualities of someone or projecting negative qualities that are not actually there on to someone or something. Once we understand this fact it will become easy to let it be. However, while we are learning this skill there are several antidotes we can apply, such as our daily review, patience and acceptance.

Patience—This is something we should cultivate. The best advice is to try and walk away from the situation that is making you angry. If we cannot do that, then we should not react straight away, but should first try counting to ten and spend a little time reflecting on the situation. This will give us the space to calm down and see things more rationally. Of course, this is not a simple thing to do when one is wrapped up in the moment, and this is where patience comes in. The most hurtful things are said in the heat of the moment, so defuse that moment with patience. There is no evil like anger, and no courageousness like patience.

Acceptance—This is accepting that people are the same as we are. Everyone is struggling to find their way in life. We strive for happiness, and so does everyone else. If we think in this way, a feeling of warmth and compassion will arise in us. If we are compassionate towards others, it is harder to get angry at them. This, again, is something you can think about in your daily review sessions.

We have to understand that we are all in this together. We are confused, trying to make sense of the world, discontented with life, and desperately searching for peace of mind, so what can be gained by getting angry with other people? The anger we show towards others directly affects us. There is an old Zen story about this. One day the Master asks his student, 'Tell me, if you buy a gift for someone, and that person does not take it, to whom does the gift belong?'

The student answered, 'It would belong to me, because I bought the gift'.

The Master then said, 'That is correct. And it is exactly the same with your anger. If you become angry with me and I do not get insulted, then the anger falls back on you. You are then the only one who becomes unhappy, not me. All you have done is hurt yourself.

'If you want to stop hurting yourself, you must get rid of your anger and become loving instead. When you hate others, you yourself become unhappy. But when you love others, everyone is happy'.

Reflection

1. Think of the last time you became angry with someone. Try to bring up the emotions you felt at the time. Just sit with those feelings for a while. What were the consequences of your anger? Did the anger benefit you or the other person?
2. Think what the consequences would have been if you had let the anger go. Again, sit with those thoughts. After doing this reflection I believe you will be able to see that your emotions are in turmoil when you are angry, and this is not a rational state to make decisions in. If by doing this reflection anger has arisen in you, sit quietly for a few minutes and simply watch your breath go in and out, and let the anger be.

Unawareness

Unawareness is a lack of understanding of the true nature of things, which leads us into wrong views. In the Avatamsaka Sutra, Gautama Buddha stated:

'Because of their unawareness, people are always thinking wrong thoughts and always losing the right viewpoint and, clinging to their egos, they take wrong actions. As a result, they become attached to a delusive existence'.

As we are unaware of the true nature of the world, we start clinging to objects, people and ourselves, which leads to wrong actions and causes us to grow attached to our perception of reality.

So what exactly are we unaware of? There are three main things we are not aware of, or if we are, it is only on an intellectual level: impermanence, nonself and cause and effect.

The belief that things are permanent leads us to become attached to sensual objects. This in turn leads to endless suffering when things change, break or die. I am not just talking about material objects here, but also about people, religions, the weather, countries, sporting teams and so on. This will be fully discussed in principle 36.

Our strong attachment to a fixed and solid sense of self also leads us into unending suffering. Even though we know we are made up of innumerable parts, we still think of ourselves as being a solid, permanent thing. This causes great suffering for us when we become sick, grow old or are nearing death. We are so attached to this sense of self that we cannot even face the fact that we are someday going to die. This will also be fully discussed in principle 36.

If we plant a rice seed we are going to get rice if the conditions—such as soil, weather and so on—are good. What we most certainly will not get is a banana, because the causes and conditions are not correct for a banana to grow. So everything comes into being through a series of causes and conditions. This is another thing we are unaware of.

It means your actions have consequences. If you spend your time being horrible to everyone around you, people are not going to like, respect care for you. This is true for any of our actions of body and speech. So if we understand that there are consequences, we are more likely not to do wrong or harmful actions.

In order to reduce our suffering and stop ourselves getting attached to a delusive existence, we have to become aware of impermanence, nonself and causes and conditions—not just aware intellectually, but make these three things our driving force. Let them be behind all of our thoughts and actions. Only then can we dispel our unawareness.

Reflection

1. Think carefully about these three main things we are unaware of. Are you just aware of them intellectually? Do they cause you to suffer? If so, in what way? Do you think if you made them an integral part of your life, you would be able to reduce your suffering?

So these are the three poisons that are a major part of our suffering. We have to make them part of our reality. We should not ignore them, try to control them or repress them, just understand and experience them without getting tangled up in them. In the Cula-dukkhakkhandha Sutra, a cousin of Gautama Buddha stated that even though he understood the teaching on the three poisons, they kept coming back:

> 'For a long time now, I have understood your teachings this way: "Clinging desire is a defilement of the mind; anger and aversion is a defilement of the mind; unawareness is a defilement of the mind." Yet even though I understand your teachings that clinging desire is a defilement of the mind, anger and aversion is a defilement of the mind, unawareness is a defilement of the mind, there are still times when the mental quality of clinging desire invades my mind and remains, when the mental quality of anger and aversion…the mental quality of unawareness invades my mind and remains'.

The point is that until you can experience these poisons without acting upon them, they will keep disturbing your mind and driving your actions.

Third truth—the cessation of suffering
This is usually called nirvana, and there are some very mystical and romantic notions of what it means. I am sure you will have your own opinion on this topic. For me, as I

have stated previously, I do not believe we can totally end our suffering, but we can reduce it considerably. I believe this because suffering is woven into the very fabric of our lives. As stated in the first truth, our suffering starts at birth and continues till our death. This is what Gautama Buddha stated in his first discourse: 'Birth is suffering, ageing is suffering, death is suffering'. So my understanding is that it is not going to be possible to end the suffering, only reduce it.

It doesn't matter what your belief on this subject is, as it is not going to impede your journey along this meandering path. If you believe nirvana will lead you to a promised land, or you believe suffering can be ended, or you believe it can only be reduced, that is fine. The two important points we have to be aware of are, first, we understand there is suffering in our lives and, second, we know what sort of things cause this suffering. If we embrace these two points, we are on the right track.

This third truth is showing us that there is a cure to the suffering we experience. That is the good news. Now all we have to do is find out what medicine we need to take. This is the fourth truth, and it will be covered in the next principle.

Reflection

1. Think about what you want to get out of this meandering path. Is it enlightenment, nirvana, an end to being reborn, your next life in a celestial

realm, an end or reduction of your suffering? This is your personal decision and I am not going to tell you what to want or believe. I just want you to be fully aware of what you want. That way it will be easier for you to set goals and boundaries. You will also be able to follow your progress at your daily review sessions.

33—Follow the eightfold path

The fourth truth is the truth of the path of practice. This is the eightfold path that leads to a reduction in our suffering and helps us live a more responsible life.

This path was not taught as a way to control people or as a moralistic path; it is a way to reduce the suffering caused by the three poisons. It is also not a religious path; it is a life-style practice, and so it does not require you to perform any rituals, prayers or ceremonies. You are not even required to call yourself a Buddhist, so anyone can follow this path no matter what religion they have, what country they come from or their background.

By practicing this path, you are not only helping yourself, but also the whole of society. Everything in the world is interconnected and built upon mutual support, so what we do affects others. If you lead a virtuous life, you help build a virtuous society. It further follows that if you lead a nonvirtuous life, you will create a nonvirtuous society. This is obviously quite a simplistic way of looking at it, but I think it gives you an idea of what I am trying to convey here. In the Bija Sutra it states if you plant a good seed you will get good fruit, and the same is so with the eightfold path. If you follow this path you are planting a good seed and you will be building a good future for yourselves and others.

> 'Just as when a sugar cane seed, a rice grain or a grape seed is placed in moist soil, whatever nutriment it takes from the soil and the water, all conduces to its sweetness, tastiness and delectability. Why is that? Because the seed is good. In the same way, when a person has appropriate view, appropriate intention, appropriate speech, appropriate action, appropriate livelihood, appropriate effort, appropriate mindfulness and appropriate concentration, whatever bodily deeds he undertakes in line with that view, whatever verbal deeds… whatever mental deeds he undertakes in line with that view, whatever intentions, whatever promises, whatever determinations, all lead to what is agreeable, pleasing, charming and profitable. Why is that? Because the view is good'.

The eightfold path is comprised of three aspects:

1. Seeing Clearly
   Appropriate View
   Appropriate Intention
2. Living Responsibly
   Appropriate Speech
   Appropriate Action
   Appropriate Livelihood

3. Staying Focused
   Appropriate Effort
   Appropriate Mindfulness
   Appropriate Concentration

I will take each point individually, but before I do that I want to say something about the use of the word *appropriate* in describing the eight elements of the path. The word in Pali is *samma*, and it is usually translated into English as *right* or *correct*, but I feel it doesn't capture the meaning quite accurately. The words right and correct sound moralistic and make one think in terms of right and wrong or correct and incorrect, but I believe that is not how it was intended to be. I feel *appropriate* is a much better word. Appropriate actions will lead you away from harmful acts, whereas inappropriate actions will lead towards harmful acts.

The first aspect of the eightfold path is seeing clearly, which includes appropriate view and appropriate intention.

Appropriate View
This is sometimes called appropriate understanding. So what is the view and what do we have to understand about it? The appropriate view refers to the four truths, and what we need to understand are the workings of cause and conditions.

Gautama Buddha mentioned appropriate view first in the eightfold path because, if we set off with an inappropriate view, we are liable to go down the wrong path. It would be the same as going on a long journey to somewhere you have never been before without a map or GPS. If you set off without knowing what direction you need to go in, you are very soon going to get lost. It is the same with the eightfold path: if you start off with an inappropriate view, you are very soon going to get lost, confused and disillusioned.

So if we have an appropriate view, the rest of the eightfold path should also be much clearer. Instead of confusion and disillusion, we will obtain clarity and understanding. It will help us to see that our suffering stems from our mind, and the reduction in our suffering also stems from the same mind—they are different sides of the same coin.

It is important to fully understand and implement the four truths. In the Magga-vibhanga Sutra it states:

> 'And what is the appropriate view? Knowledge concerning suffering, knowledge concerning the causes of suffering, knowledge concerning the stopping of suffering, knowledge concerning the way of practice leading to the stopping of suffering: This is called the appropriate view'.

As I have stated in the previous principle, we have to first become aware of the suffering running through our lives. This is the starting point. We then need to become familiar with the causes of this suffering. After that, we have to realise that there is a way to end or at least reduce our suffering. This will lead us to the eightfold path. This is the first part of having an appropriate view.

The second part of this view is to understand the working of cause and conditions.

From what I have written previously in this book, it should now be obvious that our actions have consequences, which means whatever we do and say will become a cause for our future conditions. I am not talking about future lives here; I am talking about this life. We are the architects of our future. This is how we should be thinking. We should not be thinking that our lives are conditioned by some system of reward and punishment meted out by an outside force. This way of thinking is just shirking our responsibilities. Of course, it is easier to blame someone else for our problems, but this will not help us bring about a change for the better in our lives.

Gautama Buddha in the Anguttara Nikaya stated that:

> 'People are the owners of their actions, the heirs to their actions; they come from their actions, are tied to their actions, and are supported by their actions. Whatever intended actions they do, good or bad, of those they shall be heirs'.

If we act in a kind, caring, helpful and compassionate way, we are building a good future for ourselves. I am not talking about some metaphysical law here. I am just stating the way life is. If we act in a bad way by not caring for others, stealing, lying, cheating, killing and generally acting in a harmful way, people are not going to want to be associated with us or help us when we need it. This is the way of the world. But if we are the opposite kind of person, people are more likely to feel kindness and compassion towards us, and will be willing to help when we need it. Also, if we are a kind and caring person our conscience will be clear and this will also reduce our mental suffering.

There is no scientific evidence for this, but just look at your own experiences and I am sure you will see that your actions have consequences. If you kill someone you will be caught and sent to prison or put to death. However, if you are not caught, you will have to carry the torment, anguish and guilt around with you for the rest of your life. Either way there are consequences for your act of killing.

Having said that, I am not suggesting that if you act in a good way the whole of your life is going to be rosy. Unfortunately, that isn't going to happen, but it will reduce the chances of bad things happening. It will also put you in a better frame of mind to be able to cope with these unfavourable situations when they arise.

When we have the appropriate view regarding cause and conditions, it encourages us to live a virtuous life. This is a life where we take responsibility for our actions because we know it is going to affect our future and the future of all the people we come into contact.

Reflection

1. Think carefully about causes and conditions. Look at situations in your life where you have done good acts and received good consequences. You can also look at times when your acts were not helpful, and see what the results of these acts were. It is important that your understanding of cause and conditions comes from your own experiences.

Appropriate Intention

Once we have the appropriate view, we will be ready to start moving along the path. The next element of the path is appropriate intention. What I am talking about here is your motivation. It is our conditioning that moves us into doing something with our bodies, speech or minds.

Appropriate intention is divided into three sections: letting be, freedom from ill will and harmlessness.

Letting Be

Sometimes this is talked about as renunciation, giving something up, rejecting, or abandoning, but I think a better way to describe this is the act of letting be. What we are trying to let be is attachment to, or craving for, sensual objects.

I believe renunciation is never going to work. The more we try to renounce something, the more we get ourselves entangled in it. As long as you are fighting something, you are giving it power. You give it as much power as you are using to fight it. So in that way renunciation will not work. This is why I say let it be, because by doing that you are giving it no power and it will simply disappear on its own.

Letting be does not mean that you have to live your life as an ascetic; the world would be in a greater mess if that happened. We have to personally decide what level of letting be is suitable for us.

Gautama Buddha taught that clinging to desire is one of the origins of suffering; we covered this in the section on the three poisons. Look back over what I wrote about 'clinging desires' to refresh your memory.

Just letting our clinging desires be may sound fairly easy, but when we try to let things be, a strong feeling inside stops us from succeeding. This happens because we are so attached to our family, friends and belongings. It is never easy to suddenly just let them be. Though it is not an easy thing to do, it certainly is not impossible.

If we believe sensual objects are going to give us true happiness, we will start clinging to them and this will in turn cloud our thoughts and actions. We will start seeing things as permanent and this is where our suffering will begin.

How do we let our clinging desires be? There are several ways, but I believe the best one is reflection on impermanence, which will be covered in principle 36.

It takes time to change our perceptions and it is not going to be easy, but if you don't start, you will never finish. We have to slowly start chipping away at our clinging attachment to sensual objects. This way we will be gently let things disappear bit by bit.

Reflection

1. Sit quietly and think of some material item you are attached to. Now think what it would be like not to have that item. What feelings and emotions rise in you? Sit with those for a short time. Now gently let whatever feelings and emotions you have float off. Don't chase after them; just let them be.

Freedom from Ill Will
This is when we do not have any thoughts of causing others harm. It is the opposite of ill will, which is when we wish harm upon others.

Ill will can arise when we are unhappy with someone, jealous, have too much pride, anger, have an aversion towards someone and so on. An example of this is when someone has hurt us, such as our friend, partner or family member, and we start wishing bad things to happen to them. This is not a physical action, but a mental action. It doesn't necessarily follow that we will act upon our ill will, but of course our actions are driven by our thoughts, so it is always a possibility.

Maybe you are in line for a promotion and the only thing in your way is a colleague. Out of jealousy and pride, you wish that some harm will befall your colleague so you can get the job. This is ill will based on our own selfish needs and wants; it shows absolutely no regard for anybody else's thoughts and feelings.

How we liberate ourselves from ill will is to foster the thought that other people, just like us, are fighting against the suffering running through their lives. They want to be free of the suffering and want only happiness. If we think like this it will cause goodwill to arise within us. So caring for others' feelings and showing them genuine warmth replaces ill will with a sense of goodwill.

Now when I talk about caring for others' thoughts and feelings, I am not talking about sympathy or pity, but real empathy. This is when we put ourselves in other people's shoes and truly understand that they wish to be treated kindly and with warmth.

When I was living in London, I found people didn't seem to have time to show any warmth or empathy for others. They were so wrapped up in their own busy lives that they didn't notice anyone outside their own circle of friends. It is like that in many cities and towns in the West. To get people to have ill will towards you was easy. Just get in their way when they are trying to board a bus or metro, and bad thoughts will arise in them instantly.

This is how life is these days. We tend to ration our kindness to people we are friendly with. This way of acting is selfish and shows why there is so much ill will in the world today.

So how do we start to build a feeling of goodwill towards others? Gautama Buddha taught us a good method called Metta Bhavana. Here is a variation of this that I have taken from my first book, *The Best Way to Catch a Snake*. It is a form of reflection on kindness and is split into three parts, which embraces three types of people: those we are friendly with, those we are not friendly with and the biggest group by far, those we do not care about one way or another. The point of this practice is to build friendliness towards all three types.

Start by doing the breathing or body scan meditations mentioned in Chapter One. This will ensure that you are relaxed and open to your feelings.

Now, start reflecting on your friends. This is the easiest way to begin because you already have a certain amount of warmth towards them. Think of a close friend and start to reflect on their positive qualities and their acts of kindness. A note of caution here: try not to use someone you are sexually attracted to because kindness could quite easily turn into lust. It is also recommended that you do not use the same person each time or else you may get attached to them.

By reflecting on your friend's good qualities and kindness, positive feelings will arise. Once this has occurred, you should move away from reflecting on your friend and concentrate on your feelings that have arisen. These feelings should be your primary focus. They should be feelings of warmth and empathy. Spend some time being aware of this warmth and see how happy and peaceful it makes you feel.

Keeping the above feelings in mind, move on to the next type of person, who is someone you dislike. Picture this person in your mind and examine him or her closely. See the person's pain, suffering, loneliness and insecurity. See that all he or she really wants is to be happy. Now start to radiate the same feelings you had for your friend towards the person you dislike. Project all the respect, warmth and kindness that you can muster.

Finally, picture a person you pass by everyday but do not care about one way or another. Again, feel this person's pain and see how all he or she is looking for is happiness. Radiate your warmth and kindness towards this person and imagine how that makes him or her feel, and in turn, how you feel.

This is a simple way of cultivating respect and warmth for everybody, regardless of whether you know them or not, whether you like them or not. Remember, though, that this is not a reflection activity that you do only in the privacy of your home. It should be applied to your daily life so that you cultivate a friendly and open attitude towards everyone without discrimination. That of course includes yourself, so if you are feeling a bit low or your self-esteem needs a boost, you can start this practice by radiating warmth and kindness towards yourself.

This is how one can build goodwill and find freedom from ill will.

Reflection

1. Do the practice mentioned above. Remember, to get the full benefit from it you will have to practice regularly. It is up to you how deeply you go into this practice;—the deeper you go, the more you get out of it—but I would suggest you start gently and work your way slowly into it.

Intentions of Harmlessness

You should now have started to have feelings of goodwill towards others. These feelings should drive you towards actions that are not harmful. Remember, our mind controls our actions, so feelings of goodwill should lead to harmless actions.

As mentioned before, everybody wishes to be free of suffering but is still gripped by discontent, anguish, unease, dissatisfaction and all other kinds of suffering.

People have their own suffering, but we should understand that we also play a part in other people's suffering by not having compassion for them, not caring for their well-being and not seeing that, like us, they are trying to free themselves from all forms of suffering.

There are various reflections that you can practice that will help you start having compassion for others. Again, I have taken this reflection from my first book. First, start by doing the breathing or parts of the body meditations mentioned in Chapter One.

Do these reflections on the three types of people mentioned in the goodwill section. However, this time choose people who you know are suffering, and radiate compassion towards them.

Again, start your reflection on a friend who you know is going through a rough time. Reflect on that person's suffering directly and then reflect on how, like yourself, your friend wants to be free from pain. You should continue this reflection until a strong feeling of compassion arises within you.

Remember, compassion is not pity or sympathy, but is a form of empathy. Pity and sympathy stem from our own emotions, which are not stable or reliable. Whereas empathy is where you put yourself into another person's shoes and feel what they are feeling. The beauty of this is that you are not projecting your thoughts and prejudices, but are actually seeing things from another person's point of view.

Once you start experiencing a strong feeling of compassion, hold onto it and use it as a standard for the other two types of people.

Think of a person you know who is suffering, but whom you dislike, and then reflect on their suffering. See the world through their eyes, try and understand what they are going through. Try to genuinely feel their pain and suffering. Once you have achieved this, start radiating the powerful feeling of compassion you felt before.

When you feel such strong compassion for a person, it is difficult to dislike them any more because you now understand that they feel suffering, just like you.

Next, think of a person you really have no feelings for one way or another. Start reflecting on how they also have causes for pain, sorrow, anguish and dissatisfaction. Again, once you have truly felt their pain, start radiating compassion towards them. This exercise helps you realise that we are all suffering the same way, and there really are no strangers in this world.

By doing these reflections, you will be able to build compassion for everyone because you will know that all of us are the same. Please note that by doing this reflection you are not going to ease another's suffering, but you are going to build your compassion for them.

Reflection

1. Now do the reflections mentioned above. Remember, to get the most from them, you should do them on a regular basis.

This ends the 'seeing clearly' aspect of the eightfold path. Remember to constantly check how you are progressing along the path. This can be done during one of your daily review sessions.

Living Responsibly
The second aspect of the path is living responsibly, which includes appropriate speech, appropriate action and appropriate livelihood.

Appropriate speech covers refraining from lying, refraining from using harsh words, refraining from using divisive speech and refraining from gossiping. All of these topics have been covered in principle 10. I would recommend you go back and familiarise yourself with them.

Appropriate action covers refraining from killing, refraining from stealing and refraining from sexual misconduct. All of these topics were covered in the five precepts in principle 9. Again, I think it would be beneficial for you to go back and read this principle one more time.

Appropriate livelihood was covered in principle 13, so go back and read it again.

The living responsibly aspect of the eightfold path shows us that it is important to remember that if we do not act in the appropriate way with our body, speech and mind, we will cause disharmony amongst the people we come into contact with. We have to integrate this part of the path into our daily lives and be mindful of what we are doing.

It would be a good idea to set yourself goals and boundaries—try not to break them or step over them. But if you do, don't beat yourself up; simply reconfirm your boundary and try again.

In your daily review, look at what you have done, thought and said during the day. Was it positive or negative? Did it cause peace or disharmony? If you acted in an unhelpful way, think of how you could have handled it better. This constant review of your behaviour will help you change and, in turn, live more responsibly.

Staying Focused
The final aspect of the eightfold path is staying focused, which is achieved by appropriate effort, appropriate mindfulness and appropriate concentration.

Appropriate Effort
Gautama Buddha has shown us this meandering path, from the Mangala Sutra, and it is up to us to follow it. However, our minds have a tendency to jump around like a child on a trampoline. So we really need to try and stay firmly focused on the job at hand. This is going to take a great amount of effort because we are easily distracted and it doesn't take much to draw us back into old habits.

We know from our own experiences that without putting in effort at school, university or work, we are not going to get on in life. We also know that is true for our relationships as well. So we need to put in great effort whilst travelling this eightfold path and the meandering path in general.

We need to train our minds to put in great effort, to ensure we are not bringing any harm to ourselves and others, and this can be achieved by the consistent application of the four great efforts mentioned in principle 19.

To summarise, the four great efforts are:

1. The effort to avoid
2. The effort to overcome
3. The effort to develop
4. The effort to maintain

As this is an extremely important teaching from Gautama Buddha and a very useful one for helping us along the path, I believe you should go back to principle 19 and read through it again.

Remember to examine these four great efforts in your daily review sessions so you can see your progress. This way you will be putting in the appropriate effort and will transform your harmful actions into helpful ones.

Appropriate Mindfulness
Mindfulness is a hot topic these days, and I fear it is going to become just another buzz word. I believe it is actually too important for that to happen. We have to be mindful, and have an awareness of, all of our actions or we are not going to reduce our suffering.

If we are not being mindful of our thoughts, we could end up doing harmful actions with our body or speech. If that happens, we will probably harm another person, which will cause them to suffer, and from this our suffering will grow. This is what I mean when I say we have to be totally mindful in order to reduce our suffering.

We have to be mindful of what we are saying, which is appropriate speech. We have to be mindful of our body actions and their impact, which is appropriate action. We have to be mindful of our thoughts, feelings and emotions so we are not falling into ill will. We also have to be mindful of the work we do and its impact on society, which is appropriate livelihood. We especially have to be mindful of the effort we are putting into ensuring all of our actions of body, speech and mind are in line with living responsibly. From this you can clearly see how important mindfulness is and why I do not wish it to become a buzz word.

When we do mindfulness meditation it is not a process of doing something; it is more about not judging, not thinking, not planning, not wishing, not imagining. All of these are just interferences, things the mind does to take control. With mindfulness we are just watching and letting be. We are watching what arises and letting the harmful thoughts, feelings, and emotions go. By doing this there is no need to cling to anything; the mind just stays in the present and does not float back to the past with all its memories, or to the future with its hopes and fears.

Gautama Buddha stated in the Digha Nikaya that there are four foundations of mindfulness:

- Mindfulness of body
- Mindfulness of feelings
- Mindfulness of mind
- Mindfulness of mental objects

Mindfulness of Body
What we are trying to do here is get in touch with our bodies. Although our bodies are so important to us—let's face it, without them we would not be here—we never take the time to get in tune with them. So this is what mindfulness of the body is all about.

There are many different types of reflections on the body:

Postures of the body—walking, standing, sitting, etc.
Reality of the body—seeing the body as a collection of parts.
Material elements—seeing the body as a physical process.

For me, the most simple and effective one is doing a full body review. This was covered in Chapter One. Go back now and do a body scan and see where your tension is, what areas you need to pay attention to, and get in tune with the different areas of your body. Remember, the point of this exercise is to become aware of your body without making any judgements.

On a day-to-day basis this means that whatever you do with your body affects you and everyone around you. So by staying mindful of the actions of our body, we reduce the risk of causing any harm.

In your daily review you should look back and see what actions you have carried out with your body. The ones that are conducive to responsible living should be noted. This will ensure that, with enough repetition, they soon become spontaneous. The ones that are not conducive to living responsibly should also be noted, and a clear effort should be made not to do them again. This can be done by rehearsing, during your review session, a better way to have acted, so in the future you will naturally act in a different way. It is through staying mindful of the actions of our bodies that we will be able to live responsibly.

Mindfulness of Feelings
This is sometimes called mindfulness of sensations, but here I will stick with the word feelings. There are three types of feelings: pleasant, unpleasant and neutral, and one of them is present during every moment of our experience. They underpin every single moment of our lives. You may not be aware of them because they can be strong or weak, but they are always present.

We should be mindful of our feelings, and check in on a regular basis. If we leave our feelings unchecked, pleasant feelings can lead to clinging desire and attachment, unpleasant feelings to anger or aversion and neutral feelings to unawareness. We can check in at work when we have a quiet moment, at home or wherever we are able to set a few minutes aside. It doesn't take long to see how we are feeling. If we are feeling unpleasant, look at why that is. What is causing it? Once you know what the cause is, you can just let it be and not engage with it. If you do engage with it, it will grow bigger; do not repress it as that is going to make matters worse later on. Acknowledge that you have this feeling and let it be on its merry way. If you have a neutral feeling, be careful; it could be you are not showing compassion or are actually not present in the moment. If it is a pleasant feeling, enjoy it but don't get attached to it because, as you know, it isn't going to last.

It takes time to train ourselves to check in like this, so another good time to look at our feelings is during our daily review session. When you are looking back over the day, choose one situation and see what feelings that invoked. Did it bring up pleasant, unpleasant or neutral feelings? Don't try and control the feelings, just be mindful of them. Once you are more skilled in doing this, you will be able to see what feelings usually arise in what situations. This will allow you to not get dragged back to the past or pushed headlong into the future.

Reflection

1. Think of something that just happened to you within the last hour. Note if the feeling you got from the event was pleasant, unpleasant or neutral. Just watch in a detached way, do not think in

terms of 'this painful feeling is happening to me', or 'that pleasant feeling is mine'. Watch the feeling arise and then disappear. Stay in the present moment and not in the past or the future—just stay mindful.

Mindfulness of Mind
This is about looking at the mind as though we are looking in a mirror: just observing what goes on, but not trying to change anything. We have to look in a dispassionate way and ask ourselves, 'How is the mind at the moment? Is it full of clinging desire, anger or aversion, unawareness? Is it present in the moment or distracted?' We should look at the mind in this way; do not pass any judgement, just look at what is going on as though we are observing something outside of us.

Do not see the mind as 'your' mind. Look upon it as something that is present, but with no self attached to it. This is not an intellectual exercise, and you are not required to form any ideas or opinions. It is just a simple process of discovery.

By observing the mind and seeing the thoughts, feelings and emotions come and go, we can see how they just appear and are quickly gone again. We start to observe patterns and see how one type of thought follows another. We become better at knowing ourselves and understanding what is driving us.

If you observe hateful, sad, unpleasant thoughts, don't ignore them, struggle against them or try to repress them. Just observe them. Don't be frightened, worried or try to chase them off. Stay focused, observe what arises and let it be.

What we are trying to do is recognise every thought as it arises. So if a happy thought arises, we just recognise it as a happy thought. If an unhelpful thought arises, we recognise it as an unhelpful thought. Don't let any thought arise without recognising it, and don't try to change or fix it. Be completely nonjudgmental and let the thought go. We have a tendency to try and change the world, but with this practice we learn to cultivate the ability to be relaxed with what is going on. By letting be, the mind becomes free and we gain a sense of peace.

This way of observing our thoughts isn't just something we do for an hour a day on the meditation cushion. We have to take it into our day-to-day lives. If a helpful thought arises, act on it; if an unhelpful thought arises, let it be. This way we are not going to indulge in harmful acts, only kind and helpful ones.

We rarely stop and spend time on observing our minds. We just let thoughts, hopes, fears and dreams come and go unchecked. We don't think twice about devoting a lot of time and effort on our clothes, belongings, family, friends or beautifying our bodies, but we leave the mind uncared for. So it is time to start caring for the mind, as it is the one thing that can bring about a great change in our lives.

In the Adanta Sutra, Gautama Buddha stated this about the mind:

'I know not of any other single thing that brings such woe as the mind that is uncultivated, uncontrolled, unguarded and unrestrained. Such a mind indeed brings great woe.

'I know not of any other single thing that brings such bliss as the mind that is cultivated, controlled, guarded and restrained. Such a mind indeed brings great bliss'.

Reflection

1. Sit quietly and do a mindfulness of breathing or a body scan. Now start observing the mind. What thoughts are arising? Is the mind full of clinging desire, anger or aversion, unawareness? Is it alert, distracted, tense or relaxed? Whatever it is, simply be aware of it.

As I stated before, mindfulness of mind isn't just for the meditation cushion. You have to learn to observe the mind moment by moment. You can also observe it during your daily review, but remember to be dispassionate and don't try to change things—observe and let be.

Mindfulness of Mental Objects
This foundation is called mindfulness of mental objects because everything around us exists for us as mental objects. They are what they are because that is how we recognize them. What we gain from this practice is the awareness of the interconnectedness of all things and

their temporary nature. We see that they are without self-essence and are conditioned by everything else.

Gautama Buddha taught several methods of mindfulness of mental objects: the mental objects of the five hindrances, four truths, six internal and external sense bases and five aggregates. What we have to ensure is that we understand these mental objects are not mine, not I, not self, but we just see them as phenomena.

When we begin to be mindful of mental objects of the five hindrances, which were covered in Chapter One, it helps us take responsibility for our lives and leads us to the ten helpful acts. So we have to be aware of when these hindrances do or do not arise. When ill will is present in us we know, 'There is ill will present in me'; or while ill will is not present in us, we know, 'There is no ill will present in me'. We also know how the ill will that has not yet arisen comes to arise; we know how the ill will that has arisen comes to be discarded. This is how it is explained in the Satipatthana Sutra. So it is important to know how the mental objects of the five hindrances arise and their antidotes, which you can find in Chapter One.

Mindfulness of the mental objects of the four truths makes us aware that this is suffering, this is the cause of the suffering, this is the cessation/reduction of the suffering and this is the path leading to the cessation/reduction of the suffering. So we have to be aware when suffering has arisen, know its cause and how to reduce it. This will help us steer clear of suffering and encourage us to follow the eightfold path.

We use mindfulness of the mental objects of the five aggregates as an analysis of five constituents to dispel the idea of a self. We will cover these aggregates and nonself in principle 36.

There are six internal and external sense bases. The internal senses are eye, ear, nose, tongue, touch and mind. The external senses are visible objects, sound, smell, taste, tactile objects and mental objects, such as ideas, hopes and dreams. We have to perceive the six internal and external bases as just that: six internal and six external bases. We should see them as not mine, not I and not self. They are just impermanent and unsatisfactory phenomena. It is because we think they are permanent, satisfactory and are going to bring us lasting happiness that we suffer. So we must be mindful of these sense bases and the suffering that comes with them.

Reflection

1. Choose one of the mindfulness of mental objects above and spend time reflecting on them. See how they are not you, are not permanent and only bring suffering.

This brings us to the end of appropriate mindfulness. If we are going to be mindful we have to be fully aware of, but not tangled up in, our bodies, feelings, minds and mental objects. By being mindful, we will be able to take full responsibility for all our actions, which will go some way to reducing our suffering. These four mindfulnesses will ensure that our minds become calmer and we are present in the moment, but not engaged with it. Being mindful means we are conscious of every thought, feeling, emotion and action.

Appropriate Concentration
Traditionally, what is talked about in appropriate concentration is being able to concentrate single-mindedly on an object of meditation. However, I feel that before we can get to that point, we need to learn about single-minded concentration on our actions of body, speech and mind.

There is good and bad concentration. An assassin about to kill his victim, a soldier on the battlefield, a burglar breaking into a house, these all act with a concentrated mind, but their concentration cannot be characterised as appropriate as they lead to harmful actions. What is appropriate is concentration that leads to a wholesome state of mind.

So what is appropriate concentration? Gautama Buddha stated in the Maha-Cattarisaka Sutra that appropriate concentration is dependent on the development of all the preceding seven steps of the eightfold path:

> 'Now what is appropriate concentration with its supports and requisite conditions? Any singleness of mind equipped with these seven factors,

appropriate view, appropriate intention, appropriate speech, appropriate action, appropriate livelihood, appropriate effort and appropriate mindfulness, is called appropriate concentration with its supports and requisite conditions'.

So appropriate concentration means a state where all mental faculties remain centred on one particular object or point.

While concentrating on appropriate view, you have to stay focused on cause and effect. Whatever intentional actions you do—be it with your body, speech or mind—will create a reaction in the future. You have to be naturally aware of this fact whenever you perform any intentional action. You also have to stay focused on the impermanence of everything, or you may find yourself getting attached to things, which in turn will cause you to suffer. We tend to have a fixed and solid sense of self, which is not an accurate view. This again is going to cause us suffering in the long run.

Next, you should concentrate on appropriate intentions. Our intentions should be to help and not harm ourselves and others. To achieve this we have to remain centred on what is motivating us. We have to ensure our mind isn't being driven by any of the three poisons or is clouded by ill will, because if it is, our actions of body and speech will reflect that and we will end up harming someone. By reflecting on what motivates you, it will ensure you do not intentionally harm yourself or others.

Now we come to concentration of appropriate speech. A lot of the time we open our mouth before engaging the brain, and because we are not focused, what comes out can be harmful, unkind and unhelpful. We lie, use divisive speech, use harsh words and gossip with such ease, it is frightening. It is as if our mouth has a life of its own. To counter this we have to concentrate on our speech. Lying is never going to help anyone. When we use divisive speech we are not making friends; we are just causing divisions between people. Using harsh words to someone's face is going to hurt them, and gossiping is a waste of time. So we have to have the appropriate level of concentration towards our speech, and then we will learn to talk in a way that is both helpful and kind.

Concentration of appropriate action is where we direct our attention towards the actions of our body. This will ensure we refrain from killing, stealing, sexual misconduct and other harmful actions of the body. Gautama Buddha advised his son, Rahula, to reflect on any deeds he is thinking about carrying out in this way: Is the deed going to cause harm to himself or others? If so, do not do it, as it is a bad deed entailing suffering. However, if you reflect on the deed and it is going to be helpful to yourself or others, or at the very least, not harmful, you should do it again and again, as this is a good deed entailing happiness. Thus, we must be sure we are fully in tune with our actions, so that we are aware of when we are helping or harming others.

This brings us to concentration of appropriate livelihood. We have to ensure our work does not bring harm to anybody. We may be doing a dangerous job and if we do not concentrate on our actions, we may bring harm to someone.

Whatever we are doing we have to be sure we put in the appropriate effort and appropriate mindfulness. If we do not concentrate our effort on all of the steps in the eightfold path, we could become lazy or distracted, and this could lead to us harming someone or something. If we do not focus our mind on the present moment, it may lead our thoughts to drift back to the past or jump forward to the future. Neither of these is helpful. By concentrating on the present moment our minds will be calm and our actions kind and helpful.

The appropriate concentration is where we stay totally concentrated on all aspects of the eightfold path

Reflection

1. Think about the first seven steps of the eightfold path. Do you give them your full concentration? If not, does it lead to unhelpful mental states arising? When you remain focused on all the steps of the eightfold path, does it help calm your mind and aid you in carrying out helpful and kind acts?

Following the eightfold path is not easy because many of the things we have to let be are very dear to us. We are addicted to them and have probably spent an awful lot of time cultivating them. Letting these unhelpful things just be can disturb us. Therefore, the act of letting be takes diligence, discipline and full concentration. We have to understand each of the eight steps and then implement them. They have to become a part of our lives, as only then will our minds be at ease and we will be able to reduce our suffering and see through the craziness in this world.

34—Work towards freedom from suffering

I have mentioned various ways of reducing our suffering throughout this book, so now I want to discuss things that may stop us from reducing our suffering, namely, the ten fetters. These are ten things that shackle us to a life of suffering. If we cut through these fetters, we will be able to start reducing our suffering. So what are these ten fetters? It states this in the Sanyojana Sutra:

> 'There are these ten fetters. Which ten? Five lower fetters and five higher fetters. And which are the five lower fetters? Self-illusion, doubt, grasping at rites and rituals, clinging desire and ill will. These are the five lower fetters. And which are the five higher fetters? Passion for form, passion for formless, conceit, restlessness and unawareness. These are the five higher fetters. And these are the ten fetters'.

The first of the ten fetters that chain us to suffering is self-illusion. This is the belief that we are permanent, unchanging and solid beings. This leads to the illusion of a separate self, which we get attached to, defend, cherish and spend lots of money on glorifying. It makes us egotistic, arrogant, proud and conceited. This is a major obstacle to reducing our suffering. As I have stated previously, I will discuss this in principle 36.

The second fetter is doubt. What we are talking about here is having doubts about Gautama Buddha's teachings and practices. It is a state of mind where nothing we hear or see satisfies us. It's when our expectations do not match our experiences. It may lead us to become perplexed and confused.

Now, doubt shouldn't be looked upon as a bad thing, as it can encourage us to investigate deeper and help clear up our confusion. The problem comes when our doubts are not satisfactorily resolved, and at that point they become a hindrance, as discussed in Chapter One.

If, after much questioning and investigating, you still have extremely strong doubts about Gautama Buddha's teaching and practices, I would suggest it is perhaps a good time to reevaluate whether you are following the right path for you. When there is doubt in your practice that cannot be resolved, this can bring you up against a brick wall. It is better to walk away than to try and carry doubt into your practice.

The third fetter is grasping at rites and rituals. This isn't saying we shouldn't use various practices to help us reduce our suffering, such as mindfulness practice, because these are very helpful. What it is saying is that we shouldn't get attached to rites and rituals, or have the wrong view about them, such as thinking they have some magical power.

Our attachment to rites and rituals is as problematic as our attachment to sense objects and people, or anything else for that matter. Rites and rituals are the coming together of causes and conditions, which makes them impermanent. So, by clinging to them, we are actually causing ourselves more suffering, not less.

We have to understand that by grasping at a certain rite or ritual we are not going to be miraculously transported to a better place or become a Buddha. That simply isn't realistic. Purification does not come about by washing yourself in a holy river, paying monks to do prayers for you, or adopting some form of extreme asceticism. We actually have to do the practice for it to work. Think of it this way: you are sitting by the river and you want to cross it, but there is no bridge or boat. However, there is wood, nails, hammer and so on laying on the ground, so you could make the effort and construct a boat to cross the river. Instead, you decide to sit there and pray—do you think you are going to get to the other side by reciting prayers? No, and neither did Gautama Buddha. Instead, he emphasised the importance of making individual effort in order to achieve our goals. He stated in the Ittha Sutra that if we want to attain things, we have to follow the path of practice:

> 'These five things are welcome, agreeable, pleasant and hard to obtain in the world. Which five?

> 'Long life, beauty, happiness, status and rebirth are welcome, agreeable, pleasant and hard to obtain in the world.
>
> 'Now, I tell you, these five things are not to be obtained by reason of prayers or wishes. If they were to be obtained by reason of prayers or wishes, who here would lack them?
>
> 'It's not fitting for the disciple who desires happiness to pray for it or to delight in doing so. Instead, the disciple who desires happiness should follow the path of practice leading to happiness (the eightfold path). In so doing, he will attain happiness'.
>
> (The same applies to the other four agreeable things.)

To free ourselves from the shackles of this fetter, we have to practice with diligence and make sure we do not get attached to any rites and rituals. We also need to, once we have studied a teaching, examine its purpose. This will ensure we do not wrongly grasp at its meaning, as this could bring us more harm and suffering. In the Alagaddupama Sutra, Gautama Buddha gave this advice to the monks:

> 'There are here, monks, some foolish men who study the teaching; having studied it, they do not wisely examine the purpose of those teachings. To those who do not wisely examine the purpose, these teachings

will not yield insight. They study the teaching only to use it for criticising or for refuting others in disputation. They do not experience the true purpose for which they ought to study the teaching. To them these teachings wrongly grasped, will bring harm and suffering for a long time. And why? Because of their wrong grasp of the teachings'.

Fetter four—clinging desires—has been covered earlier in this chapter; fetter five—ill will—has been covered in Chapter One under the five hindrances.

Fetters number six and seven are concerned with becoming attached to form and formless realms, respectively. When we are attached to the form realm, we want to be reborn as a human; when we are attached to the formless realm, we wish to be reborn in another world system. The point is that any attachment, be it to this world or another world, is going to impede our progress along the path to reducing our suffering. As this is a secular book, I think readers have probably suspended their belief in rebirth or other realms until there is some clear and demonstrable evidence. However, that is not a problem; what we need to gain from these fetters is that attachment to anything is only going to set us up for more suffering.

The eighth fetter is conceit. This is where we think ourselves superior to others, we have a superiority complex. We also believe ourselves to be right. We may listen to others' views, but as we know better and are never swayed by them.

When I first came to India and did the rounds of Buddhist teachings, I was submerged into the world of the Dharma bums. They would sit around for hours and brag and boast about their practice and the high teachings they have had. They would say things like, 'I've had hundreds of empowerments', 'I know so-and-so guru very well', and 'My meditation practice is secret and I can't talk about it'—even though they did. They were so conceited, it made it hard for me to even listen to them much of the time.

I understand that we are all different and we do different practices, but if we talk in a conceited way, it is going to hinder our practice. We will end up with more suffering. So the answer is to be humble. If you ask someone something, do it out of curiosity and not pride. I dislike people talking about how wonderful their practice is and how much better it is than anyone else's. I find someone who is proud and conceited very difficult to be around.

Restlessness is the ninth fetter. This is an overexcited, distracted, confused, worried and uneasy state of mind. It is a mind that is not at peace or tranquil; it is the opposite of the one-pointed mind that we aim for in our meditation practice.

It is caused when we allow our mind to be worried about something in the past we cannot change, or concerned about something in the future that hasn't happened yet. So, of course, the antidote to this is being mindful and present in the moment.

The final fetter is unawareness, which has been covered earlier in this chapter. It means not understanding that we are suffering, the causes of this suffering and the path out of this suffering. It also means not knowing that our actions have consequences, that things are impermanent and that there is no solid and lasting self. Look back over the section on unawareness just to remind yourself, because this fetter is very powerful as it makes us go through life seeing things in an unrealistic way.

All of these ten fetters are things that shackle us to a life of suffering. If we are going to be able to reduce our suffering, we have to be aware of these fetters and apply the appropriate antidotes.

Reflection

1. Think about these following questions: Are you attached to an illusionary image of self? Do you have doubt about the effectiveness of Gautama Buddha's teachings? Are you attached to certain rites and rituals? Do you have clinging desire? Is your mind poisoned by ill will? Are you attached to this, or any other, world? Do you find yourself acting in a conceited way? Do you feel restless and worried? Are you ignorant about suffering, impermanence and whether our actions have consequences? Give these questions a lot of thought. If you have any of these fetters, work on the antidote. This will ensure they do not become an obstacle that will prevent you from reducing your suffering.

Remember, you can always revisit these questions during your daily review session. This will help you map your progress.

35—Be unaffected by worldly conditions

Nobody's life is perfect, we all have good and bad days. This is part and parcel of worldly conditions. Sometimes the world is like a rose, all beautiful and fragrant. Other times it is like the stem of the rose, all thorny and prickly.

An optimist will see the world as rosy, whereas a pessimist sees it as thorny. But realistically, the world is both rosy and thorny. A person who understands this point will not be seduced by the rose, or become averse to the thorns. Gautama Buddha taught that there are eight worldly conditions, and a realist will understand that the pendulum swings both ways; sometimes they will be under the sway of the four desirable conditions, and sometimes under the sway of the four undesirable conditions.

We have to accept that these eight worldly conditions are part of this human life. So what are the eight worldly conditions? The desirable ones are gain, status, praise and pleasure. The four undesirable ones are loss, obscurity, reproach and pain. It doesn't matter if we see them as desirable or undesirable as they are all causes of our suffering.

We are all subject to gain and loss, not only of material things such as money, but also of our friends and family. We may go out to buy a 3D television and it makes us very happy, until one day it is stolen and we then become sad—gain and loss. If you are a businessman, you suffer from gain and loss on a regular basis. You may have, in the past, met a wonderful person who you got on really well with, but who recently died—gain and loss. These are some examples of what we are subject to in our lives.

Status and obscurity are two worldly conditions that confront us in the course of our daily lives. Status comes in various forms, such as celebrities and politicians, or you may be highly regarded within your profession, or even a well-respected Buddhist teacher. Whatever the status, you can become attached to your public image and the prestige that goes with it. Even if we do not want to be famous, we still like to be looked upon in the best possible light. I am sure, if we are honest, we all like a bit of status, because who wants to feel unimportant or overlooked?

The next pair of worldly conditions is praise and reproach. We all like to be told, 'Well done!' when we do something right. It makes us feel happy and gives us a sense of pride. Praise is like some sort of drug we quite happily get addicted to. Whereas no one enjoys being reproached, even if they have done something wrong.

The final pair is pleasure and pain. This is where we are the same as animals: we chase after pleasure and run away from pain. I do not know anyone who prefers sorrow to laughter, or harm to happiness. This is just the way we are. It is a bond that ties us all together.

Who do these eight worldly conditions apply to? Is it just people who are not well versed in Gautama Buddha's teachings? Is it for people who are not practicing mindfulness? Actually, they apply to all of us. So then you are probably going to ask, 'What is the difference between a person who practices this path and a person who doesn't?' This is what it says in the Lokavipatti Sutra, which is aptly translated in English as 'The Failings of the World':

> 'For an uninstructed run-of-the-mill person there arise gain, loss, status, obscurity, reproach, praise, pleasure and pain. For a well-instructed disciple of Gautama Buddha there also arise gain, loss, status, obscurity, reproach, praise, pleasure and pain. So what difference, what distinction, what distinguishing factor is there between the well-instructed disciple of Gautama Buddha and the uninstructed run-of-the-mill person?'

The distinguishing factor between these two is the way they handle the worldly conditions. This is what the sutra says about how a person not instructed in Gautama Buddha's teachings acts.

> 'Gain arises for an uninstructed run-of-the-mill person. He does not reflect, "Gain has arisen for me. It is inconstant, stressful and subject to change." He does not discern it as it actually is'.

(It is the same when loss, status, obscurity, reproach, praise, pleasure and pain arise.)

'His mind remains consumed with the gain. His mind remains consumed with the loss...with the status... the obscurity...the reproach...the praise...pleasure. His mind remains consumed with the pain.

'He welcomes the arisen gain and rebels against the arisen loss. He welcomes the arisen status and rebels against the arisen obscurity. He welcomes the arisen praise and rebels against the arisen reproach. He welcomes the arisen pleasure and rebels against the arisen pain. As he is thus engaged in welcoming and rebelling, he is not released from birth, ageing or death; from sorrows, lamentations, pains, distresses or despairs. He is not released, I tell you, from suffering and stress'.

So an uninstructed person doesn't reflect on worldly conditions. He welcomes them and gets consumed by them. A person who is well instructed does the opposite of this:

'Now, gain arises for a well-instructed disciple of Gautama Buddha. He reflects, "Gain has arisen for me. It is inconstant, stressful and subject to change." He discerns it as it actually is'.

(It is the same when loss, status, obscurity, reproach, praise, pleasure and pain arise.)

'His mind does not remain consumed with the gain. His mind does not remain consumed with the loss…with the status…the obscurity…the reproach…the praise…the pleasure. His mind does not remain consumed with the pain.

'He does not welcome the arisen gain or rebel against the arisen loss. He does not welcome the arisen status or rebel against the arisen obscurity. He does not welcome the arisen praise or rebel against the arisen reproach. He does not welcome the arisen pleasure or rebel against the arisen pain. As he thus abandons welcoming and rebelling, he is released from birth, ageing and death; from sorrows, lamentations, pains, distresses and despairs. He is released, I tell you, from suffering and stress.

'This is the difference, this the distinction, this the distinguishing factor between the well- instructed disciple of Gautama Buddha and the uninstructed run-of-the-mill person'.

So how we react to, and reflect on, these eight worldly conditions is what's important. If we respond to gain in a clinging, grasping way, we are acting like the run-of-the-mill person mentioned in the sutra. But if we reflect on the gain and see it as an impermanent and fleeting thing, we are not going to bring suffering upon ourselves. This is because we understand that loss is going to follow the gain, as sure as day follows night.

I am sure we have all dreamt of our fifteen minutes of fame, and there is nothing wrong with that. Some people are world superstars and others are just well known in their own backyards; but whatever your status, it is important to see it as a fleeting thing. Very few people stay famous all of their lives, for most it is only a few years. So to hold on to fame as though it is something tangible is going to bring you suffering.

When we reflect on our status and obscurity, we will be able to see that they are just projections and not solid or permanent. This releases us from the suffering they can cause.

If we are able to face reproach in an impassive way and remain calm even though people are saying hurtful things about us, then we are dealing with this worldly condition in a proper way. If we give very little regard to whether we are held in high esteem or thought of as a person of no influence, then we can be said to be rising above worldly attachments.

If we are able to keep our composure when we lose out, or are glorified as being a very special, talented person, this is the sensible thing to do, even though it is not always that easy. Here our daily review is invaluable. We can look at how the mind reacts to praise and reproach and, in fact, all of the eight worldly conditions. This gives us a chance to investigate these conditions in a calm, more relaxed manner.

It is human nature to soak up praise and push away reproach. I know when someone says something nice about me I feel happy and proud, but if I am reproached, I get defensive and hurt. Through reviewing these states of mind we can understand them as one and the same: impermanent and fleeting. This will help us let them go, and in turn, reduce our suffering.

Watching pleasure and pain arising in the mind, and remaining open to them without attaching to or rejecting them, enables us to let the conditions be, even in the most emotionally charged circumstances.

I believe we all strive for pleasure and push away pain, even animals. Pleasure is what we aim for in life and not pain. But they are both things that come into being for a short time and then disappear, so in that respect they are no different. Gautama Buddha's advice is to not welcome them or rebel against them, just let them arise and go.

When we start seeing the eight worldly conditions for what they are, and watching the mind's reactions to them, we will be able to prevent them from causing us to suffer. This is not just a meditation or daily review practice; we have to take it into our day-to-day lives. We have to understand that life is full of gain, loss, status, obscurity, reproach, praise, pleasure and pain.

Someone is always going to profit and someone else will lose out; for every famous person, there are hundreds of others who are unknown; if one person is reproached, another will be praised; and what gives one person pleasure, will give another pain. This is the way of the world. It doesn't matter if you are skilled in Gautama Buddha's teachings or not. You will still be subject to the eight worldly conditions. It is how you deal with these conditions that differentiates you from others.

Reflection

1. Spend time reflecting on gain, loss, status, obscurity, reproach, praise, pleasure and pain. See what feelings and emotions arise. See the ones you are attached to and the ones you repel. Remember, do not welcome or rebel against the feelings and emotions that arise, just be aware of them, acknowledge them and then just let them be on their way.

Do not forget to look at these eight worldly conditions in your daily review. If one of these conditions arose during the day, look at how you reacted to it. See that by getting attached or having feelings of aversion, you are causing yourself to suffer.

36—Understand impermanence and nonself
These are two of the most important topics Gautama Buddha taught. In the *Dhammapada,* verses 277, 278 and 279, it states this:

> 'All conditioned things are impermanent'
> 'All conditioned things are unsatisfactory'
> 'All things are nonself'

...when one sees this with wisdom, one turns away from suffering. This is the path to purification.

So let's look at impermanence first. What things are impermanent? Gautama Buddha said this in the Alagaddupama Sutra:

> 'You may well take hold of a possession, monks, that is permanent, stable, eternal, immutable, that abides eternally the same in its very condition. But do you see, monks, any such possession?'—'No, Lord'.—'Well, monks, I, too, do not see any such possession that is permanent, stable, eternal, immutable, that abides eternally the same in its very condition'.

So it is clear from this stanza that nothing remains without change. Why is that? Well, all phenomena are made up of two or more parts and come into existence through a series of causes and conditions.

Gautama Buddha taught that there is no phenomenon that exists from its own side—that is, there are no phenomena that are not compounded.

Things do not just come into existence by sheer magic or by some superior power, such as a god. It is through causes and conditions, the joining together of things, that phenomena come into existence.

Everything is dependent on other things. When we fill a jug with water, it is not the first drop that fills it, nor the last drop; it is each drop individually coming together that fills the jug.

When we plant a seed in the ground, it will not just miraculously grow. It needs water, sun, nutrients from the soil and so on, or it will not grow. So it grows when these causes and conditions come into play. We come into being when sperm meets with an egg. We don't just miraculously appear or are made by some god; it is through various causes and conditions.

When things come together, something comes into being. They last a while, even though they are constantly changing, and then they disintegrate. This is the true nature of all phenomena and it is because of this everything is impermanent.

Let's look at some examples of what is impermanent. The universe is impermanent. Planets explode and black holes keep forming—all this is a display of impermanence.

Let's look closer to home, to the earth. We are all aware of how the earth is changing, mainly because of our own actions. A thousand years ago the earth was a very different place. Innumerable species of animals have since become extinct, other species have evolved, forests have disappeared and lakes have dried up, while so-called human civilisation grows dramatically. This is due to impermanence.

The weather changes constantly, and time does, too. Seasons change and, quite important, so do our thoughts and feelings. Absolutely everything around us is changing and impermanence is a far-reaching factor in our lives. Why don't we embrace it?

Even though we nearly all understand impermanence on an intellectual level, we choose to ignore it. It is much nicer to believe things will last forever. This simply isn't the case, however, and all we are doing is setting ourselves up for future suffering.

We struggle against impermanence because we get too attached to things, get so involved and wrapped up in them. We fool ourselves into believing that something we like will last forever. When it doesn't, we are surprised and start suffering. But this idea that things will last forever is a delusion.

Let's look at an example of our attachments to something and how it makes us suffer.

You see an advertisement on television for the latest smartphone. You then search the Internet to check out the specifications. Your excitement grows. Your anticipation is high. When the product arrives in the shops, you rush to buy it. One hour later it's in your hands and you are playing with it. The more you look at it, the more you see how indispensable it is, and you become convinced that it is the one thing that can bring you true happiness in life. You can't think of anything else, and you wonder how you ever lived without it. You spend the next few weeks proudly showing it to your friends, who envy you for having it. Every time you look at it, a sense of pride fills you. You are so happy—your life seems complete. Then the inevitable happens: a newer, faster, smaller and more powerful version comes out. You hold the smartphone in your hand, but your happiness has turned to discontent. Why is that? Gautama Buddha taught us that all sense objects, including those fashionable, technical gadgets, are impermanent. There is no happiness inherent in them; we simply project happiness onto these objects. So when our thoughts toward the object change, or the object changes itself, the suffering kicks in.

That is the type of impermanence we do not like. On the other hand, if we are experiencing hard times, we are only too glad that things change. We may have gone out last night and this morning we have a headache. That will eventually go and we will start to feel better. We may have had a serious illness, but things change and we survived it and we are happy. Perhaps we have just separated from our loved one and are now going through a bad time; when that ends we will be more than happy. If we have just lost our job and are now facing financial hardship, we will of course be extremely pleased to find new employment. So impermanence is not all bad news.

Our view of impermanence can become quite selective. We don't seem to fully understand the nature of impermanence, and seem not to even spend time thinking about it. We need to make the understanding of impermanence a part of our lives and our very way of thinking. To do this we must reflect on it, but before we can do that we need to understand why Gautama Buddha taught this and what the benefits are.

So why did Gautama Buddha teach us this? In order to stop us from grasping at things. If we understand that phenomena only come together through causes and conditions, and thus do not exist by themselves, we will not get attached to our friends, family or belongings. So if we are not attached to them, it follows that we are not going to suffer once they have changed or gone.

What is the benefit of knowing about impermanence? There are many, but a major one is that it helps us focus on our lives and on setting goals so we don't waste the precious little time we have on this earth. This is using impermanence as a motivational tool. If we just stop and think for a moment, how much time do we waste in a day? We manage to waste time in so many different ways. Without knowing it, the days turn to months, the months into years and before we know it, we will be on our deathbeds full of regret.

Impermanence helps us realise that we and all our friends and family will eventually die. We don't know how, where and when, but we do know it will happen. If we are not attached to them, we are not going to suffer once they depart.

If we understand impermanence, knowing the thing we hold dear is going to change, we are less likely to get attached to it, and if we are not attached, when it changes we will not suffer.

I will let Gautama Buddha have the last word. This is how he spoke about impermanence in the Sukhavativyuha Sutra:

> 'Nothing in the world is permanent or lasting; everything is changing and momentary and unpredictable. But people are ignorant and selfish, and are concerned only with the desires and suffering of the passing moment. They do not listen to the good teachings nor do they try to understand them; they simply give themselves up to the present interest, to wealth and lust'.

Reflection

I have been traditionally trained in Buddhism, and one thing I was taught to do was reflect upon death. Now I know this may sound morbid and even a little strange, but I can tell you from my own experience that it really works. It works on so many levels. First, you understand impermanence and start to let go of your clinging attachment to things. Second, you become motivated to make the best of this life. And third, you will not be fretting about death. In the West, talking about death is such a no-no. Why is that? We can learn so much from reflecting upon it.

Below I have written four reflections on different aspects of death. Please do not get distressed; just work through them slowly. These are taken from the traditional Buddhist practice and may be too much for you to reflect on here. If so, do them during one of your daily review sessions, but I do strongly recommend you try them.

1—Think that nothing lasts

Think that this year will soon be gone; last year has already gone; each year departs so quickly. Think about the world and all its inhabitants, and how they are impermanent. Think about how you have gone from a baby to a child to an adult, and realise that you are heading towards death. Think of how every day, week, month and year brings you closer to your death. Reflect upon these points. This is not to depress you; it is to make you understand that everything is impermanent and the time to try and reduce your suffering is now.

2—Think about how many other people have died

Think about all the people you have known who have died. Some have been older, some younger and some the same age. There have been so many! Think about how most people, even though they are surrounded by impermanence, have died unprepared. Think of the times that you have been shocked to find out about someone dying, even though you are surrounded by impermanence. Read the papers and watch the news, count how many people have died or been killed today. Reflect on these points and understand that death is all around us, and let this fact motivate you to be a better person.

3—Think of the many causes of death

Think of the numerous circumstances that can bring about death: heart attack, illnesses, accidents, falling down the stairs, being hit by lightning—the list is endless. We do not know when, where and how we are going to die. What we know is that death will come. As we don't know our fate, we should spend the precious time we have engaging in practice. Reflect on these points and don't let your death be a surprise.

4—Reflect what will happen at the time of death

If you have misused your life and spent most of it indulging in unhelpful actions and being consumed by clinging desire, anger or aversion and unawareness, at the time of death you may be terrified. You are not going to be able to calm your mind, and it will run riot. It may be that you imagine all kinds of scary situations and will be afraid of losing your family and friends. You may even worry about the money you are leaving behind. It is not possible to relive your life once you reach death, even if you are full of regret and remorse, so don't allow yourself to get to that point.

• • •

Now let's look at nonself. This is a difficult subject for many of us to grasp because we have invested so much time and effort into building and reinforcing a sense of self. However, Gautama Buddha stated that what we call a self is just a coming together of different parts. In the Vajira Sutra a woman goes to the woods to meditate. Whilst she is there her mind gets distracted and these questions arise:

> By whom was this being created?
> Where is the living being's maker?
> Where has the living being originated?
> Where does the living being cease?

These are questions we all grapple with at some time in our lives. However, she doesn't get distracted by these thoughts and thinks to herself:

> 'This is purely a pile of fabrications. Here no living being can be pinned down. Just as when, with an assemblage of parts, there's the word, car, even so when aggregates are present, there's the convention of a being'.

The questions are presupposing there is a self, but that is just a fabrication. Some people think we are our thoughts, but thoughts come and go, so we are not our thoughts. Others believe we are our bodies, but scientists tell us that millions of cells in our body are renewed every minute, so that by the end of seven years we don't have a single living cell in our body that was there seven years before. Our bodies are changing, so we can't be our bodies. So who are we?

No lasting, permanent self can be pinned down because we are just a collection of parts, much the same as a car. When various parts are assembled, we label it a car, and the same for us. When all the parts come together, we call it a self. As this self is compounded it follows that it is impermanent, and so it will come together, remain for a period of time and finally die.

We have to be careful here that we don't misunderstand what is being said. Gautama Buddha was not saying there is no self or there is a self. The question of there being a self or not is just a 'thicket of views', and one should avoid such ways of thinking. This isn't because he couldn't answer the question, but that it had no bearing on easing our suffering. These types of questions get us confused and may lead us down the wrong path, such as nihilism or eternalism. The point he was making was there is no permanent, solid self. We are just a coming together of various parts.

The reason for this teaching was to stop us clinging to a self, because that clinging or attachment will lead to conceit, which will in turn lead to us suffering. He taught three different types of conceit we have to be aware of:

1. Thinking we are better than others, which causes the seven types of pride: pride of ego clinging, simple pride (thinking you are special), pride of thinking we are better/greater than others, pride of pride (thinking you are the best in the group), pride of thinking we are only slightly inferior to an outstanding person, perverted pride (when we are proud of something that is not good), and blatant arrogance.

2. Thinking we are worse than others, which leads to envy or resentment.
3. Thinking we are the same as others, which can lead to us being complacent.

So the next question that may come to mind is, 'If there is not a permanent and solid self, how do we experience the world?' I see, hear, smell and so on, how is that possible? I have a wife, family and job, so if there is no self, who has all of these things?

Gautama Buddha stated the way we experience the world is through five aggregates. The five aggregates come together through a series of causes and effects, and then we experience the world around us. When the five disperse, we stop experiencing the world—in short, we die. What are these aggregates? In the Maha-punnama Sutra lists them this way:

> '...these are the five clinging-aggregates, i.e., form as a clinging-aggregate, feeling...conception...mental formation...consciousness as a clinging-aggregate'.

So the aggregates are form, feeling, conception, mental formation and consciousness.

Form includes our bodies and the material objects that we encounter. This aggregate includes both internal and external matter. It is the only aggregate that represents material things. The remaining four aggregates represent mental phenomena.

Feelings are divided into three parts: pleasant, neutral and unpleasant. These experiences can be mental or physical. There are six kinds of experience, five physical and one mental. These experiences arise when your eyes come into contact with objects, your ears with sound, nose with smell, tongue with taste, body with tangibles and mind with thoughts and ideas.

Conception is where we attach a name to the experience and categorise it by shape, colour, location, sex and so on. These concepts we were either born with or have learnt. We pick up concepts from our parents, friends, society, teachers and other social groups. It should be noted that our whole world is built on concepts, judgements and ideas, and not on objectively existing realities, as is commonly believed.

Mental formation is where we respond to an object of experience. It stems from an impression created from previous actions, which makes us respond in a certain way. These responses have moral consequences as they can make us act in a skilful, neutral, or unskilful way.

The final aggregate is consciousness. This is where we get an awareness of an object. If an eye comes into contact with a visible object, the eye consciousness will become associated with the object and visual consciousness will arise. If the nose comes into contact with a smell, the nose consciousness will become associated with the smell and the olfactory consciousness will arise. The same goes for the remaining four consciousnesses.

So let's put this all together. Your eyes see a form. Your consciousness becomes aware of it. Your conception identifies it. A pleasant, neutral or unpleasant feeling arises. Your mental formation makes you respond to it with a conditioned reaction. This is how the five aggregates work together to give us a personal experience.

You should keep in mind that these aggregates do not constitute a self; they are just the way we experience the world. Gautama Buddha explained this point in the Anatta-lakkhana Sutra:

> '…any kind of form whatever, whether past, future or presently arisen, whether gross or subtle, whether in oneself or external, whether inferior or superior, whether far or near, must with right understanding how it is, be regarded thus: "This is not mine, this is not I, this is not myself."'

And the same goes for the other four aggregates.

These aggregates are compounded and so are impermanent and ever changing, so how can they constitute a self?

So nonself means there is no permanent, solid self. We come into being through a series of causes and conditions, and we experience the world through the coming together of the five aggregates. These five aggregates also come into being through causes and conditions, so they are impermanent and ever changing. In the Kalakarama Sutra prologue it states this about the aggregates:

> Form is like a mass of foam
> And feeling—but an airy bubble.
> Conception is like a mirage
> And mental formations a plantain tree.
> Consciousness is a magic-show,
> A juggler's trick entire...

Reflection

1. Reflect on these profound questions: Am I my body? Am I my thoughts, feelings and emotions? Am I the five aggregates? Am I permanent? Who am I? These are questions we will probably not be able to fully answer, but they are good to ponder as they show us that we are not who we believe we are.

As impermanence and nonself are such important subjects, inasmuch as they can help reduce our suffering if we understand them, we should constantly contemplate them in our daily review sessions.

37—Free yourself from defilements
In the dictionary, *defilement* means a state of being polluted, and that is what we are talking about here: our

minds being polluted. So what is polluting our minds? It is destructive mental states, and these are what we need to remove so we can free our minds.

You do not have to study Gautama Buddha's teachings for very long to understand that the very heart of his teaching centres around the mind. Sometimes the essence of his teachings is reduced to three points:

> Help everyone;
> If you cannot help, at least do not harm them;
> Calm your mind.

These three points form a graded sequence of steps that leads you from an external practice to the essential internal practice. If we want to reduce our suffering, we cannot do it just by knowledge and meditation alone. We need to live a responsible life by understanding that we do not live in a vacuum and our actions have an effect on others, as their actions have an effect on us. We should look upon Gautama Buddha's teachings as a bird. On one wing there is ethics, and on the other there is the calming of our mind. The bird cannot fly with just one wing and, likewise, we cannot reduce our suffering with only one part of the teachings.

This is what Gautama Buddha said to his monks in the Vatthupama Sutra regarding defilements of the mind:

> 'Monks, suppose a cloth were stained and dirty, and a dyer dipped it in some dye or other, whether blue or yellow or red or pink, it would take

the dye badly and be impure in colour. And why is that? Because the cloth was not clean. So too, monks, when the mind is defiled, an unhappy destination may be expected.

'Monks, suppose a cloth were clean and bright, and a dyer dipped it in some dye or other, whether blue or yellow or red or pink, it would take the dye well and be pure in colour. And why is that? Because the cloth was clean. So too, monks, when the mind is undefiled, a happy destination may be expected'.

Why is a simile of a soiled piece of cloth used in this discourse? It is because the cloth is naturally pure, so it is possible to remove the dirt by washing it, as it is not permanently stained by the dirt. The same can be said for our mind. The defilements have not permanently stained our mind; they have just temporarily polluted it. The defilements can be cleansed, but as with cleaning the cloth, it will take effort on our part. However, before we can start cleansing our minds we have to first understand that our minds are defiled, as Gautama Buddha stated in the Pabhassara Sutra:

'Luminous is the mind. And it is defiled by incoming defilements. The uninstructed run-of- the-mill person doesn't discern that as it actually is present, which is why I tell you that—for the uninstructed run-of-the-mill person—there is no development of the mind.

'Luminous is the mind. And it is freed from incoming defilements. The well-instructed disciple of Gautama Buddha discerns that as it actually is present, which is why I tell you that—for the well-instructed disciple of Gautama Buddha—there is development of the mind'.

Before I talk about what the defilements are I must point out that we are not trying to stop the defilements from arising; I believe this is not possible, or even desirable. We are also not trying to repress them either, as that again will not be desirable. What we are aiming at here is being aware of the defilements when they arise and having a strategy to deal with them. I will talk more on this later.

Depending on what book you are reading, defilements can range from three to one hundred and eight. The three defilements are known as the base defilements and are clinging desire, anger or aversion and unawareness—the three poisons. What I want to go through here are the ten defilements. These form the basis for all the other defilements.

Briefly, the ten are:

Clinging desire—holding on to sensual objects, thinking they are going to bring us permanent happiness.
Anger or aversion—getting thoughts of hatred towards others and discriminating against certain people and material things.

Unawareness—not understanding the concepts of impermanence, nonself and cause and conditions.

Conceit—believing yourself to be better than others.

Wrong views—thinking things are permanent, there is a solid and lasting self, and believing whatever you do will not have any consequences.

Doubt—when something does not seem to agree with your experiences.

Torpor—inactivity resulting from lethargy and lack of vigour or energy.

Restlessness—when your mind is hopping about like a demented frog and cannot settle on anything.

Shamelessness—behaviour marked by a bold defiance of what is considered right and proper.

Recklessness—the trait of giving little thought to danger towards yourself or others.

The defilements arise in our mind and, if we want to reduce our suffering, we need to focus our work on the mind. As these unhelpful mental states run beneath the surface of our stream of consciousness, we have to exert sustained effort to be aware of them when they start to arise.

The process of becoming aware of the defilements starts with self-understanding, and we can do this in our daily review sessions. Before we can work on the defilements we must first learn to know them, to notice them at work penetrating and influencing our day-to-day thoughts and lives. In today's world we strive for instant results, but this is not possible with the defilements. It takes patience, time and perseverance. We have to systematically understand each defilement, what the consequences of them are, and then work out a strategy where we can let them be without engaging with them. Luckily, there are antidotes for each of the defilements and I have listed some below, but it has to be noted that different things will work for different people. So this is just a list of suggestions.

- Clinging desire—see that everything is impermanent and so our happiness with the sense object is not going to last. If we love someone and we get attached to them, when they want to move on, we suffer. Just enjoy your time with the person while you can, but understand that one day it will come to an end.
- Anger or aversion—when we let anger and aversion arise they lead us into inappropriate speech and action. We have to understand that in these states of mind nobody wins. It is better to walk away or not let yourself get involved in the situation.
- Unawareness—we have to study and reflect so that we understand the concepts of impermanence, nonself and cause and conditions. It is no good just intellectually knowing these three key concepts; we must reflect on them so they become a part of our lives.
- Conceit—if we believe ourselves to be better than others, we are going to lack compassion as we will not care for what others think or feel. We are actually denying others their opinions because we believe our opinions are more valid. We will also not be

making ourselves very popular as conceit is not a good trait to have. So listen to others with an open mind and welcome their point of view. This way we will not become conceited.

Wrong views—First, if we see things as permanent we will suffer when they change. So understand that all things are impermanent. Second, if we think we have a solid and permanent self, we will waste our time and money on pampering it and trying to reinforce this sense of self. This will make us suffer when we become old or sick. See that this body is just a vehicle to carry us through this life. It is made up of innumerable parts and so is impermanent. Whatever we experience in this world is not through a sold self, but through the five aggregates. Finally, we have to see that any action we take is going to have a consequence. This will steer us towards helpful actions and away from harmful ones.

Doubt—this can really eat at us if we do not resolve it satisfactorily. When doubt arises ask questions, reflect on it, look in books or on the Internet for answers, whatever is best for you; don't just leave it as it will grow and eventually become a real obstacle.

Torpor—when we allow this to take hold we become lazy and cannot be bothered with anything. If you start to feel like this, take a walk, splash cold water on your face, have a break. Again, it is for you to see what works best, but do not just follow the torpor or you will end up a couch potato.

- Restlessness—usually we get restless when our minds are stuck in the past or drifting off to the future. It may be caused by stress or anxiety. The best thing to do is a breathing or body scan meditation. This will relax you and bring you back to the present.
- Shamelessness—this behaviour shows that you really do not care for yourself. It could be that you have low self-esteem or have reached a low point in your life. If you leave this unchecked it could lead to an addiction, such as alcohol or drugs, and even may land you in prison. You need to look at the cause of these feelings of self-worth. You may need to seek professional help, such as a therapist.
- Recklessness—when our thoughts are of a reckless nature, our actions will also be of the same nature. This is dangerous for you and those around you. As with the defilement above, you really need to find the root cause of this behaviour. Having compassion for others will help here, as you will be able to see that your actions may bring harm to them.

During your daily review, look at a situation where a defilement arose. See what caused the situation to arise. After a while you will begin to see patterns emerge. Certain defilements associate themselves with certain situations. Armed with this information, you will be able to apply the appropriate antidote. What we are aiming at is to be able to spot the defilements when they arise and deal with them. As I said before, we are not ever going to stop them and we shouldn't try to repress them. Just spot them and apply the antidote.

If we are not aware of the defilements, they will arise and we will unwittingly follow them. Remember what I have spoken about all the way through this book: first we think and then we act. Keeping this in mind is the key to reducing our suffering.

Reflection

1. Look at each of the ten defilements and see which ones arise on a regular basis. Look at what situations make them arise. Then see what antidotes you have used in the past. This is just a simple reflection so you can understand the importance of the defilements. The main work will need to be completed on a regular basis during a daily review session.

38—Achieve lasting peace and true happiness

I do not want to mislead you here, so I will say at the outset that I do not think *lasting* peace and *true* happiness are achievable. Of course, we can gain peace of mind, but as we know from experience, it isn't going to last forever—nothing is permanent and this includes peace. Happiness is a relative thing and so it is impossible to say what is true happiness and what is not. What makes me happy will probably not make you happy, and so this is why I feel true happiness is misleading. A lot of the time our happiness is wrapped up in someone or something else. We stupidly think if our parents, partner, friend or boss changes we will be happy. That would be like going to a doctor with an illness and him prescribing medicine for our friend. We do seem to want to change everyone and everything around us, but leave our own thoughts, feelings and emotions unchecked.

Change has to come from within us, and in that way I believe peace of mind and happiness are within our grasp. However, they are not permanent, and so we have to continually work on them.

In the previous principle we dealt with mental states that pollute our minds, but in this principle we will be looking at four qualities of mind that we are able to cultivate in order to reduce our suffering and become more connected to the world around us.

The four states are commonly known as the four immeasurables: goodwill, compassion, appreciation and equanimity.

Traditionally, they are taught in the order I mentioned above. However, I believe the fourth one should come first. In Buddhism equanimity is not only seen as being steadfast of mind under stress, but also as an interconnectedness with everyone. Thich Nhat Hanh (Vietnamese Zen Buddhist monk) describes, in *The Heart of the Buddha's Teachings*, the Sanskrit word *upeksha* as meaning 'nondiscrimination and an even-mindedness'.

So let's start by looking at equanimity. Our lives are full of ups and downs. If we can face the downs as well as the ups, we will be able to cultivate an open and calm mind. It is easy to face the ups, but not so easy to come to terms with the downs; but if we don't, all we are doing is adding to our suffering.

When we look at the world we can clearly see how hard it is to attain a balanced mind, as we are continuously in a flux of rises and falls. These lift us up one moment and fling us down the next. This is true for everyone; we are all the same. So if that is the case, why do we discriminate against others? We are all in the same boat, all riding the same waves of life.

So equanimity is where we do not distinguish between our friends, the people we dislike or strangers, but regard everyone as equal.

This is not easy because when we are not being mindful, we are constantly being tossed around by our prejudices and emotions. So we need to have a complete openness to our experiences, without being carried away with reactions such as I like this and dislike that, or I love you and I detest you. A balanced mind will mean we are not going to be disturbed by the eight worldly conditions.

What we are trying to do here is remove the boundaries between ourselves and others by discarding our discriminations. What we are not doing is becoming detached or feeling indifferent to others. This is a common misunderstanding of what is meant by equanimity in the four immeasurables.

We have to look upon others as our equals and see that they have their ups and downs just like us. If we can do this, equanimity will be able to grow.

In principle 33, under the heading of 'Intentions of harmlessness', I gave a mediation practice that would help us see everyone as equal. What I want to do here is introduce a practice we can use while we go about our daily lives. When you feel your prejudices coming to the surface, have a set phrase to mentally repeat to yourself something like, 'They are no different than me. They, like me, are subject to the eight worldly conditions. We are all equal'. It is better for you to have your own phrase as it will resonate with you. By mentally repeating your set phrase you will stop your discriminations in their track. After a while we will naturally see all as equal, but that is going to take time. So for now, use your set phrase.

The second immeasurable is goodwill. This is the thought that we want the best for all beings, without discriminating between the people we like and those we dislike. Sometimes our goodwill only covers people that are useful, pleasing or amusing to us. This is not how we should divide groups of people; we have to see people through the eyes of equanimity. We must open our hearts to everyone, and that includes the people who make us angry, politicians from a party we disagree with, religious leaders that have different beliefs than ours, people who act and dress differently than us, and those who just have the knack of rubbing us up the wrong way. All of these people deserve our goodwill, and so we have to train ourselves to think only good thoughts about them.

We have to include ourselves in this. Sometimes we are more harsh with ourselves than we are with others. If you can't love yourself, how are you going to love others?

If we just watch our thoughts for a few hours, it becomes quite apparent that this isn't how we usually think. Not every thought radiates goodwill to others, so how can we cultivate this goodwill? In principle 33, under the heading of 'Freedom from ill will', I gave a meditation practice that will help you cultivate goodwill.

Here is a practice to use in your day-to-day life. I find the best antidote to judging someone, when we are not on our meditation cushion, is to have a set phrase that resonates with you, something like, 'May my mind be at ease, may you be happy, may everyone be free from suffering'. This phrase can be used when you feel ill will rising in you.

I remember a few years ago, when I travelled to work by metro, I would see the same man every day. I didn't know anything about this man, but as soon as I saw him I would start thinking negative thoughts. It was totally irrational and I knew that, but it just seemed to happen automatically. I spoke to my teacher at the time, and he told me to try having a set phrase ready for when I encountered this man again. The next time I saw him, I mentally recited my phrase and I started to see the man in a different light.

After reciting my phrase for a few days I never had the negative feelings again.

The next time you start to judge someone, mentally recite your phrase and your judgement will start to dissolve. Remember, we all share this planet and we all want to be happy, so the best way to end our judgemental thoughts is to wish goodwill to everyone.

You may think that this is too simple to work, but what I would say to you is try it.

Compassion, the third quality, is an understanding that the world is full of suffering, and a heartfelt wish that this suffering will come to an end or at least lessen—for ourselves and others.

Some people are so wrapped up in their own world of suffering that they forget to have empathy for other people's suffering. We seem to live in a selfish world in which people close their eyes and ears to the constant stream of tears. We seem to be able to watch the news or read the newspaper in a dispassionate way. The horrendous suffering that is going on throughout the world doesn't touch us. We have our own problems to deal with. This is not a kind or helpful way of thinking. This is not the type of world we should wish to live in or leave for our children. If we do not have compassion for others, why should they have compassion for us?

Through compassion, the fact that everyone is suffering remains vivid in our minds. Sometimes we may feel that we are not suffering, even though on some level we are. This should not stop us from having compassion for those who are suffering. Compassion should be ever present—not just for family and friends, but for everyone, even people who are acting in an unhelpful way. Once we start to discriminate who should have your compassion and who doesn't deserve it, true compassion is lost. Everyone is suffering, so everyone deserves it.

Again, the best way to ensure that compassion arises in you is to do the meditation mentioned in principle 33, or have a set phrase ready to mentally recite once you feel you are not caring for another person's suffering, something like, 'May I be released from my suffering, may they be released from their suffering, may all beings be released from suffering and may compassion arise in my heart'. But, as before, it is important that you decide on your own wording so it resonates with you. This is only a suggestion.

Sometimes when we are being harassed by a homeless man, annoyance arises in us instead of compassion. Next time that happens, mentally recite your set phrase. It doesn't mean you are going to give that person all your money out of compassion, but it does mean you will feel empathy towards him. You should recite your phrase every time you feel that you are not being compassionate. What these phrases do is connect us to others. We appreciate that they are suffering just like us, and once we have this connection, it is easier to radiate compassion towards other beings.

We should see compassion as a verb and not as a noun. It should be something we do and not just talk about or pray for. After spending many years going to Buddhist teachings, I grew very tired of being preached to about compassion. Yet when I observed the teacher, I didn't see much evidence of it being put into action. It is beneficial to reflect on compassion, there is no doubt about that, but it is far more beneficial for all concerned if it comes off the cushion and goes out into the community.

We have to be intelligent with our compassion. It is of no benefit to give money to drunken homeless people. They are just going to spend it on more drink, compounding their problems. It is far better to give them food, or to give your money to a homeless shelter that helps these people. Compassion isn't just about giving; it's about giving sensibly, and that could include money, clothing, food, your time and so on. In a nutshell, compassion is the humane quality of understanding the suffering of others and wanting to do something to alleviate it.

The fourth quality is appreciation. What we are appreciating is the happiness someone else is experiencing. With this quality we feel real joy at their happiness. The operative word here is real. It shouldn't be forced or faked, but real heartfelt joy. This is the perfect antidote for envy, which is a feeling of grudging admiration and a desire to have something that is possessed by another. Sometimes we begrudge people their happiness and feel resentment at seeing their success. This feeling of appreciation deals a killer blow to envy.

Happiness is fleeting, so to begrudge what little joy people can find in their lives is a very selfish and unhelpful quality. What we need to do is rejoice when happiness comes another's way.

When I was at school I never did very well in exams. When my friends passed their exams with flying colours, I used to feel real resentment. But who was I harming? The answer to that is myself. These negative feelings are only going to pollute one's own mind, and as we have seen throughout this book, if your mind is polluted, your actions will follow in the same vein.

Later in life when I was still rubbish at passing exams, I used to think how happy my friends would feel by passing, how their parents are going to be proud, and what a good future my friends were going to have. These thoughts of appreciation are far more constructive, and this is what we are looking for here.

So in this quality, instead of having a set phrase ready, you should think of the joy and happiness the other person is feeling and rejoice in it. By thinking this way a warm feeling grows in your own heart that leaves no room for envy.

Sometimes we take joy in another's misfortune. If we radiate appreciation towards others, we will not have these awful thoughts.

Once we have a steadiness of mind, we will have thoughts of goodwill, gain compassion and appreciate the happiness others are experiencing. These are the four immeasurables. They are called immeasurable because, by cultivating them, we are helping to reduce the suffering of an uncountable number of people. We have to persevere with these immeasurables so they become a natural way for us to think and not just a passing mood.

Reflection

1. Look at each of the immeasurables and see if you have equanimity, goodwill, compassion, and appreciation for others. I expect you will see that sometimes you do and sometimes you don't. Think of the set phrases that work best for you and then put them into practice.

Summary

Now that you have come to the end of the refining principles, you should have a much clearer understanding of what things are polluting your mind—such as the ten defilements, ten fetters and eight worldly conditions—and have an idea of how you can best deal with them. You should now know why it is important to adhere to the eight precepts at least once a month, as this will help you build self-restraint. You should understand that there is suffering in your life and what the main causes of this suffering are. You will also know what path to take so you can reduce this suffering, namely, the eightfold path. You should have a clear understanding of two of the most important teachings from Gautama Buddha: impermanence and nonself. Finally, you should know how to become more connected to the world around you by following the four immeasurables.

There is a lot to take on board here, so I would advise you to go back over this section to ensure you have fully understood it all.

9
The End of the Road

CONGRATULATIONS! YOU HAVE reached the end of the meandering path and you are now enlightened. Your certificate is in the post. Well, not quite, but you have reached the end of this book and should now be able to start reducing your suffering and begin living a more responsible life.

We have covered a lot of ground and, I hope, learnt a lot of things. But remember that these things will all stay as intellectual knowledge if you don't reflect on them, start implementing them and review your progress on a daily basis.

I strongly believe that if you start a daily review, your life will change for the better. It is a simple but profound process. It will not take any preparation and certainly will not take too much of your time. You can decide when and where you do it. All I would suggest is that you do it every day and that you be honest with yourself.

This daily review isn't a replacement for your meditation practice; it is a complement to it. So please do not stop whatever practice you are doing. Just introduce the review into your daily routine—even better, introduce it into your life.

It is extremely important that your life becomes your practice, and your practice becomes your life. What I mean by this is that the meandering path has to be about how you live your life on a day-to-day basis.

It has to be about your thoughts and actions, your relationships and how you interact with the world around you, your intention and your motivation. What we have to do is live our lives as peacefully as possible, and we do this by not causing harm to ourselves and others.

What this meandering path isn't about is future lives, superstitions, worshiping Gautama Buddha as some sort of a god, or getting bogged down in ceremonies and dogma. I am not saying these are wrong or do not work. What I am saying is that if you want to tread the meandering path, there is no need for such things.

Buddhism is vast and covers so many different topics, such as religion, philosophy, psychology, cosmology, medicine and so on. Buddhism means different things to different people. It doesn't make one person right and one wrong. There is a wonderful story about blind men and an elephant that excellently sums up what I am saying.

There was a certain ruler who called to his servant and said, 'Go and gather together in one place all the men of Savatthi who were born blind and show them an elephant'. 'Very good', replied the servant, and he did as he was told. He said to the blind men assembled there, 'Here is an elephant', and to one man he presented the head of the elephant, to another its ears, to another a tusk, to another the trunk, the foot, back, tail and tuft of the tail, saying to each one that that was the elephant.

When the blind men had felt the elephant, the ruler went to each of them and said, 'Well, blind man, have you seen the elephant? Tell me, what sort of thing is an elephant?'

The man who was presented with the head answered, 'An elephant is like a pot'. And the man who had observed the ear replied, 'An elephant is like a winnowing basket'. The one who had been presented with a tusk said it was a ploughshare.

The man who knew only the trunk said it was a plough; others said the body was a granary; the foot, a pillar; the back, a mortar; the tail, a pestle, the tuft of the tail, a brush.

Then they began to quarrel, shouting, 'Yes it is!' 'No, it is not!' 'An elephant is not that!' 'Yes, it's like that!' and so on, till they came to blows over the matter.

So you can see that if you approach Buddhism in a certain way, that's how it is going to appear to you.

Before I finish, I would just like to wish you all the best with your journey along this meandering path. If you have any questions or doubts, please feel free to contact me: buddhismguide@yahoo.com.

I will leave you with this final inspiring statement:

> 'Let us rise up and be thankful, for if we didn't learn a lot today, at least we learned a little, and if we didn't learn a little, at least we didn't get sick, and if we got sick, at least we didn't die; so, let us all be thankful'.

Also from the Author

BUDDHISM, WITH ITS stress on nonviolence, the 'middle path' and its promise of nirvana, finds many followers. But in today's time, it has become simply a fad for some, something to follow because their favourite celebrity is doing so. Simply wearing robes or carrying prayer beads does not make one a Buddhist; it has to be ingrained within, and should become a part of one's daily life. *The Best Way to Catch a Snake*, a three-part volume, is a beginner's guide to Buddhism for all those who want to start their journey towards nirvana but don't know how and where. It goes beyond the exotic rituals and practices that Buddhism today has become all about, and looks at the fundamental tenets that, without a knowledge of, one cannot be a true Buddhist. It elucidates the Four Seals, the Four Noble Truths, and the Four Thoughts of Buddhism in simple, jargon-free language. The author, a Buddhist monk himself, combines examples from his own experience with simple exercises to skillfully guide us through the Buddha's teachings. An easily relatable and valuable source of Buddhist knowledge, this book is a must for anyone drawn to the Eightfold Path of Gautama Buddha.

"The real beauty of all of the Buddha's teachings is that they are based on natural laws and are not fabricated. Anyone can practice them, and there is absolutely no need to buy anything especially for learning it. This is because what the Buddha taught is inside you, and only you can free this potential. All the rites, rituals and ceremonies that have been tagged onto the foundation teachings of Buddhism are just an outer religious covering."

Printed in Great Britain
by Amazon